You, Me and the World

3rd Edition
featuring SDGs

David Peaty

KINSEIDO

Kinseido Publishing Co., Ltd.

3-21 Kanda Jimbo-cho, Chiyoda-ku,
Tokyo 101-0051, Japan

First published 2024 by Kinseido Publishing Co., Ltd.

Cover design Takayuki Minegishi
Text design   C-leps Co., Ltd.

Photos
p.22 © Ingus Kruklitis | Dreamstime.com, © Louis Henault | Dreamstime.com; p.23 © Lucaderoma | Dreamstime.com, © Baloncici | Dreamstime.com; p.24 © Nonglak Bunkoet | Dreamstime.com; p.25 © Antonio Jose Jimenez Cabeza | Dreamstime.com; p.36 © LCVA | Dreamstime.com; p.37 © Neurobite | Dreamstime.com; pp.56-57 © Kseniya Ragozina | Dreamstime.com; p.60 © Jens Matthiaschk | Dreamstime.com, © Jinaritt Thongruay | Dreamstime.com, "Cabaña Motacú 2 en Chalalan Albergue Ecológico" © Rodrigo Mariaca (Licensed under CC BY 4.0 https://creativecommons.org/licenses/by/4.0/; p.66 © Feije Riemersma | Dreamstime.com; p.69 © Sjors737 | Dreamstime.com; p.71 © Peacepix | Dreamstime.com; p.73 © David Snyder | Dreamstime.com; pp.74-75 © Click And Capture | Dreamstime.com; p.75 © Lifeontheside | Dreamstime.com, © Sjors737 | Dreamstime.com; p.76 © Rrodrickbeiler | Dreamstime.com; p.80 © Digikhmer | Dreamstime.com; pp.84-85 © Trentinness | Dreamstime.com; p.87 © Anjo Kan | Dreamstime.com; pp.92-93 © Crisfotolux | Dreamstime.com; p.95 © Luca Marella | Dreamstime.com, © Garnett212 | Dreamstime.com, © Kanpisut Chaichalor | Dreamstime.com, © Luca Marella | Dreamstime.com; p.97 © Scott Wagner | Dreamstime.com; pp.98-99 © Nexus 7 | Dreamstime.com; pp.100-101 © Niccolo Pontigia | Dreamstime.com; p.102 © John Gomez | Dreamstime.com; p.103 © Olga Besnard | Dreamstime.com; p.104 "Peter Benenson" © Olga Berrios, "Craig Kielburger at We Day Waterloo 2011 with his brother, Marc Kielburger, in the background" © Siavash Ghazvinian, "Who Made My Clothes Protest" © greensefa; pp.106-107 © Elena Baryshnikova | Dreamstime.com; p.110 © Hutchinsphoto | Dreamstime.com

the United Nations Sustainable Development Goals web site:
https://www.un.org/sustainabledevelopment/

The content of this publication has not been approved by the United Nations and does not reflect the views of the United Nations or its officials or Member States.

All royalty income earned by the author from the sale of this book will be donated to organizations that are dedicated to making our world a better place.

 音声ファイル無料ダウンロード

https://www.kinsei-do.co.jp/download/4205

この教科書で ⬇ **DL 00** の表示がある箇所の音声は、上記 **URL** または **QR** コードにて無料でダウンロードできます。自習用音声としてご活用ください。

▶ PC からのダウンロードをお勧めします。スマートフォンなどでダウンロードされる場合は **ダウンロード前に「解凍アプリ」をインストール**してください。

▶ URL は**検索ボックスではなくアドレスバー（URL 表示欄）に入力**してください。

▶ お使いのネットワーク環境によってはダウンロードできない場合があります。

ⓍCD 00　左記の表示がある箇所の音声は、教室用 CD（Class Audio CD）に収録されています。

Introduction to students

You, Me and the World has been designed to help you learn English while studying about global and social issues. In each unit, you will find all or most of the following activities.

Discussion

Each unit begins with a discussion called Talking about the Topic. There is at least one discussion later in each unit. If at first you are nervous about discussing topics in English, you could think about the questions and prepare answers before class. However, the main aim of this section is to develop confidence in exchanging opinions and ideas in English without advance preparation.

Words in Context

This section presents words you may need to know for the listening section. These words are presented in a context that enables you to guess what they mean and thus develop a skill that is useful for listening, reading and spontaneous vocabulary acquisition. You can check the meanings in a dictionary later if you have any doubts.

Listening

In this section, some tasks involve answering questions and others involve taking notes on an outline. However, in real life there are usually no questions or outlines, so it is important to also practice listening and taking notes with a blank sheet of paper. Watching videos on YouTube is a great way to practice listening and note-taking, especially if you can turn off the Closed Caption function.

Read and Share

In this section, each student gets a chance to be a teacher. For each unit, there are four or five different reading passages at the back of the textbook. After forming a group, each member will choose a different reading passage. Please decide quickly, as you will need plenty of time to complete this section. The reading passages are completely out of sequence, so you can't and shouldn't read any passage other than your own while doing this activity.

There are two formats:

Presentation format

Read the passage you have chosen quietly and prepare to present and explain it (including important words that the other students might not know). Don't spend too long on preparation, because we have plenty of other things to do! When each student is ready, you will take turns to present your passages to the group. Presenters should pause frequently to allow the other students to take notes or to ask them to repeat or explain something. When the presenter has finished, the other students will try to summarize what they have found out using their notes. The speaker should provide prompts if necessary and correct any mistakes. When speaking, try to maintain eye contact. When listening, focus on what the speaker is saying and on taking brief notes.

Q & A format

Read the passage you have chosen and prepare to answer questions about it. The questions are shown in the textbook. When each student is ready, decide who will be the first to answer questions. The other students will ask the questions provided. They may ask further questions if they want additional details or clarification. Finally, they will try to summarize what they have found out.

Vocabulary Review

This focuses on your ability to produce in context the words that you encounter in the Words in Context sections. It is better to write your answers on a separate sheet of paper rather than the textbook so that you can review regularly.

Writing

Each unit has one or more writing projects that may be assigned for homework. They generally involve some kind of research. Your teacher will provide specific guidelines. However, there is one rule you must never forget: every essay or report that you write must be *in your own English*. If you want to include a few words from the original source, be sure to make this clear by using quotation marks ("........") and showing the source (e.g. According to ...).
You may be asked to present your research in addition to, or instead of, a written report.

Other sections
The following sections are included in one or more units. Instructions are provided.
Survey (Unit 1)
Consolidation (Units 5, 6 and 8)
Project (Units 3, 9, 10, 11 and 14)
Brainstorming (Units 8 and 9)
Role Play (Units 1, 5 and 7)

Keeping up to date
Global and social issues are constantly evolving and facts keep changing. For example, the first edition of this book anticipated climate change and some serious consequences. We now know it is already occurring, and the impacts appear regularly in the news. However, we also have clear targets and more options for dealing with it. Whenever you come across important new information, please check that it comes from a reliable source and then share it with your teacher and classmates.

General Tips for Listening

1 Practice every day. Start with easy tasks. You can find plenty of free practice on the internet, including many interesting videos on YouTube.

2 You can listen to English on TV and radio too.

3 When you listen to English on the internet, you can use the *pause button* on your PC or smartphone anytime to stop and repeat or think about what you heard. It is better to use the pause button many times than to listen to the whole thing many times. But you should also practice without pauses.

4 Don't try to understand every word; it is usually not necessary and sometimes it is impossible.

5 Pay attention to what the speaker is saying *now*; don't focus on what the speaker has already said.

6 Don't try to *translate* in your head. Just focus on understanding the *key points*: who did what, where & when, why ...?

7 Be an *active* listener: take notes, join in the conversation, make comments.

8 Do your listening in a *quiet place*, with no distractions, or use headphones.

9 If you like movies, try watching a movie in Japanese first and then watch it in English. Or read the book in Japanese and then watch the movie in English.

10 Try watching movies and documentaries on YouTube with and without Closed Captions or subtitles.

11 And finally: relax and enjoy listening to English!

Expressions for Use in Discussion

1 Asking for repetition or for the speaker to slow down
- Could you say that again, please?
- Sorry, could you repeat that?
- Sorry, could you speak more slowly, please?

2 Asking for clarification
- Could you explain that?
- What exactly do you mean?
- I'm afraid I don't understand.
- Could you give me an example?

3 Confirming understanding
- Do you mean ...?
- So ..., right?
- If I understand correctly, ...

4 Asking for further information
- Can you tell me a bit more about ...?
- Do you have any other examples/reasons/data?

5 Showing understanding
- OK.
- I see.

6 Checking listener's comprehension
- OK?
- Did you follow that?
- Would you like me to explain that again?
- Do you have any questions?

7 Saying it another way
- In other words, ...
- What I mean is ...
- To put it another way ...

8 Taking a turn & interrupting
- I'd like to add a comment, if I may.
- Could I add something?
- Excuse me for interrupting, but ...

9 Offering a turn
- What do you think?
- Do you agree?
- What are your views on this?
- Does anyone have a different opinion?

10 Asking opinions
- What do you think about ...?
- How do you feel about ...?
- What's your opinion of ...?
- What are your views on ...?

11 Giving opinions
- I think ...
- In my opinion ...
- I don't really care.
- I'm not really interested.
- I don't know much about that.
- I've never really thought about it.

12 Agreeing and disagreeing
- I agree.
- I think so too.
- I agree to some extent.
- That's true, but on the other hand, ...

- Really? Why?
- Oh, I wouldn't say that.
- I'm afraid I (totally) disagree.

13 Reacting
- Really? That's great/interesting/ surprising/shocking ...

14 Asking for, making and responding to suggestions
- What do you think we should do?
- Do you have any ideas/suggestions?
- How about ...?
- Why don't we ...?
- We could ...
- That's a great idea!
- That sounds good.
- I doubt if that would work.
- It might be better to ...

15 Disputing facts
- Are you sure about that?
- Really? I thought ...

16 Asking someone to back up a statement
- Really? What makes you think that?
- Can you give an example?
- How do you know that?

17 Providing support
- For example, ...
- According to ....,
- For instance, ...
- ... such as ...

18 Conceding
- I hadn't thought of that.
- That's a good point.
- Really? I didn't know that.

19 Offering a counter argument
- That may be so, but ...
- Yes, but on the other hand ...
- I take your point, but ...

20 Questioning relevance
- What does ... have to do with ...?
- Are you sure that's relevant?
- I doubt if that makes much difference.
- That's beside the point.
- So what?

21 Referring back
- As I mentioned earlier, ...
- As you've already pointed out, ...

22 Returning to the main issue
- If I may, I'd like to go back to what you said about ...
- Can we get back to the original issue?
- Let's go back to the question of ...
- I think we're getting away from the main issue.

23 Using hedging expressions when unsure of the facts
- I'm not sure, but I think ...
- I may be wrong, but I've heard ...
- If I'm not mistaken, ...

Contents

UNIT 1

WASTE AND RECYCLING

Unit Goals

In this unit, you will find out about:
- sustainable and unsustainable approaches to garbage management
- urban mining
- the merits and demerits of plastic bags

1 | Talking about the Topic

Discuss the following questions with a partner or in a small group.

- How much garbage do you and your family throw away each week?
- What could you do to reduce that amount?
- What kinds of trash can be recycled where you live?
- What happens to trash that isn't recycled?

2 | Words in Context

What do you think the words and phrases in bold type below mean? Try to guess, and then check them in a dictionary.

 Tip: You can often guess the meanings of unfamiliar words from the context.

- ☐ We should **deal with** this problem before it's too late.
- ☐ All the garbage that can't be recycled or burned is dumped in **landfills**.
- ☐ My solar panel **generates** all the electricity I need.
- ☐ **Incineration** of garbage is convenient but it causes air pollution.
- ☐ They recycle gold, platinum and other **precious** metals.
- ☐ Dumping bottles and cans in a landfill is a waste of **resources**.
- ☐ Burning trash has some advantages, but its **overall** impact on the environment is harmful.
- ☐ It's cheaper to buy imported paper than to recycle it, so recycling isn't **profitable**.
- ☐ Some people **extract** aluminum cans from garbage dumps and sell them to recyclers.
- ☐ Plastic bags have been **banned** in many countries.

A Listen and write your answers to the following questions. Then share your answers with a partner or in a small group.

1   What is the traditional approach to dealing with garbage?

_____

2   What are the advantages and disadvantages of incineration?

_____

3   Which approach is best for the environment?

_____

4   How much of San Francisco's waste is recycled?

_____

5   What helps Norway to recycle all of its PET bottles?

_____

6   What happens to most of Japan's garbage?

_____

7   What is Kamikatsucho's big ambition?

_____

8   How is it trying to achieve that?

_____

9   How did recycling support the 2020 Summer Olympics?

_____

10   What is urban mining?

_____

11   Why did many people join a campaign to ban plastic straws?

_____

12   Why are plastic bags popular?

_____

13   What was the conclusion of the BBC report about the use of plastic bags?

_____

B Present a short summary of what you have found out.

4 | Discussion

Discuss the following questions with a partner or in a small group.

Tip: We often express opinions with phrases such as: **In my opinion ...**

We can agree or disagree like this:

I (completely) agree.   I agree to some extent.   I'm afraid I disagree.

- Why is Japan's recycling rate so low?
- What do you think of Norway's PET bottle deposit system?
- Would you be willing to sort your garbage into 45 categories?
- Are there any other ways to achieve zero waste?
- How could a plastic straw end up in a turtle's nose?
- Do you think plastic straws should be banned?
- What about plastic bags?

5 | Read and Share   More about Garbage

Form a small group. Each member will choose one reading passage. Read yours carefully and be ready to present and explain it. The other members will listen and take notes without looking at the reading passages. After each presentation, they will report what they have found out. The presenter will add anything they overlooked and correct any misunderstandings.

Tip: Useful expressions:

Listeners

Could you say that again, please?   Could you explain that, please?
Could you speak a little more slowly, please?
Sorry, could you repeat your explanation about ...?

Speakers

Shall I repeat that?   Would you like me to explain that?
Do you have any questions?

The 'r's of Garbage Management

Used Electrical Appliances

Paper

Drink Containers

6 | Survey How Green Are You?

Work with a partner. Interview each other. Ask the following questions. Score your answers as shown and then calculate the total.

1 *Which of the following things do you recycle?*
   - ☐ PET bottles
   - ☐ Cans (drink and food containers)
   - ☐ Paper cartons (for milk and juice)
   - ☐ Glass jars (for jam, etc.)
   - ☐ Styrofoam trays
   - ☐ Newspapers and magazines
   - ☐ Clothes

     Award yourself one point for each 'Yes' or 'I never use these products'.: _____

2 *Do you sometimes buy*
   - ☐ second-hand goods? What? (e.g. books, umbrellas, etc.)
   - ☐ things made of recycled materials? What? (e.g. printer paper)
   - ☐ things with no packaging? What?
   - ☐ refills (e.g. for ballpoint pens, shampoo, printer ink, etc.)

     Award yourself one point for each 'Yes'.: _____

3 *Do you sometimes*
   - ☐ bring your own bag to the supermarket?
   - ☐ bring your own lunchbox or flask?
   - ☐ give away or sell books and other things that you no longer need?
   - ☐ get things repaired when they break, or repair them yourself? (What?)

     Award yourself one point for each 'Yes'.: _____

4 *Do you ever*
   - ☐ buy things you don't need?
   - ☐ buy disposable goods (e.g. cheap ballpoint pens or paper cups & plates)
   - ☐ throw away food? (Why?)
   - ☐ buy takeaway drinks with plastic cups or straws?
   - ☐ buy 'fast fashion' garments?
   - ☐ buy things that can't be safely disposed of after use? (e.g. bleach)

     Take off one penalty point for each 'Yes'.: _____

     Your Score: _____

7 | Role Play   City Garbage Policy

A   Form a small group. You are the councilors of a small city. Your city has just one landfill, and it is full. There is no space for a new one. You also have an old incinerator that emits harmful gases. A court has ordered you to close it. Decide what to do.

Tip: We can make suggestions like this:

    Why don't we ...?   **How about ...ing ...?**   **What if we ...?**

    Maybe we could ...   **Let's ...**

    We can respond like this:

    That's a good/great idea.   **That wouldn't help much.**

    I don't think that would be a good idea/effective.

Proposals

1 _____

2 _____

3 _____

4 _____

5 _____

B   Consider the advantages and disadvantages of each proposal. Finally, prepare your official statement to the local citizens.

8 | Vocabulary Review

Fill each space with a suitable word or phrase from this unit. You may need to change some words so that they fit grammatically.

1 There are no cigarette vending machines here: they were .... last year.

2 Her business used to be very .... , but now it's losing money.

3 .... means burning stuff we want to get rid of.

4 The trash in old .... includes some interesting and valuable things.

5 This machine can .... gold and other valuable metals from old smartphones.

6 This small power station .... 2,000 kilowatts of electricity a day.

7 The best way to .... PET bottles is to wash and recycle them.

8 This country is rich, due to its valuable .... such as gold and oil.

9 Nothing is more .... than life itself.

10 We should consider not only the cost of recycling but also the .... benefits for the environment.

9 | Writing

Find out about the garbage management policies of San Francisco and a large city in your own country, compare them and write a report.

Tips:

1 Be sure to choose reliable sources of information when using the internet, such as reports by government agencies (.gov), well-established NGOs (.org) and academic institutions (.edu).

2 Make sure the information is both correct and up-to-date.

3 If your sources are English (many teachers require this), the teacher will want to be sure that you wrote your report by yourself and didn't just copy it. To avoid that risk, you should
   - use more than one source
   - use paraphrase and summary
   - use "quotation marks" for any sentences that you found in the original.

4 To be absolutely sure of writing it in your own English, first take notes in your own language and use those notes to write the report.

5 Use in-text citation and references to show where your information and ideas came from.

UNIT 2

SUSTAINABLE CITIES

Unit Goals

In this unit, you will find out about:

- sustainable urban transportation
- sustainable energy sources
- sustainable waste management
- sustainable food supply
- sustainable housing
- four sustainable cities

1 | Talking about the Topic

Discuss the following questions with a partner or in a small group.

- What aspects of your town do you like (for example, good public transportation, big shopping malls, etc.)?
- What aspects do you dislike?
- What could be done to make your city or town more environment-friendly?

2 | Words in Context

What do you think the words and phrases in bold type below mean? Try to guess, and then check them in a dictionary.

- ☐ Cars **account for** almost 80% of the air pollution in this city.
- ☐ People in western countries **consume** a lot of meat.
- ☐ Air pollution is caused by **emissions** from cars and factories.
- ☐ Clean air and water are **essential** for a healthy life.
- ☐ I ride a bicycle every day because the public **transportation** here is so expensive.
- ☐ The government's main **priority** now is to create more jobs.
- ☐ A desert isn't an **appropriate** place to grow food.
- ☐ You should **ensure** that you have enough money when you travel abroad.
- ☐ We turn all waste food into **compost**, which the farmers use to grow more food.
- ☐ The city **distributed** free books about nature to all the children.
- ☐ Your **carbon footprint** shows how much carbon you add to the atmosphere each year.

A Listen and write your answers to the following questions. Then share your answers with a partner or in a small group.

1 Why is it important for cities to have their own sustainable development goals?

_____

2 How can emissions related to transportation be cut?

_____

3 What can we learn from

· Luxembourg?

_____

· Antwerp?

_____

· Pontevedra?

_____

4 What kinds of renewable energy can be produced in or around cities?

_____

5 What is the aim of the circular economy?

_____

6 What are two ways to deal with waste food?

_____

7 In what ways can we reduce the environmental impact of our diet?

_____

8 How else can a city be made more sustainable?

_____

Tip: Speakers often provide a simple explanation.

      e.g.1 **... a city should be walkable. In other words ...**

      e.g. 2 **... to avoid so-called 'food miles'. The further ...**

B Present a short summary of what you have found out.

4 | Discussion

Discuss the following questions with a partner or in a small group.

- Which of the approaches mentioned in Section 3 could make your city more sustainable?
- What other approaches can you think of?

Form a small group. Each member will choose one reading passage. Read yours carefully and be ready to present and explain it. The other members will listen and take notes without looking at the reading passages. After each presentation, they will report what they have found out. The presenter will add anything they overlooked and correct any misunderstandings.

Tip: useful language for presenters when eliciting and checking listeners' summaries:

OK, so what did you find out from my presentation?

Great!   I also mentioned ...   Right. What else did I mention?

I'm afraid that's not quite right. What I said was ...

Shall I repeat what I said?

Copenhagen

Oslo

Freiburg

Vienna

6 | Discussion

Discuss the following questions with a partner or in a small group.

- Which of the communities mentioned in Section 5 is the most sustainable in your opinion?
- What could be done to make the place where you live more walkable or livable?

Fill each space with a suitable word or phrase from this unit. You may need to change some words so that they fit grammatically.

1   The aircraft is about to take off. Please .... that your seatbelt is fastened.

2   Copies of the new curriculum were .... to all schools.

3   When hiking in summer, it's .... to carry plenty of water.

4   Despite stories about plane crashes, airplanes are actually one of the safest means of ....

5   For most 4th year students, the top .... is to find a job.

6   My new refrigerator .... much less energy than the last one.

7   If you often travel by plane, you probably have a very big ....

8   What's an .... tip to pay a taxi driver?

9   The restaurant makes .... for its roof-top garden using waste food.

10 The .... from the old incinerator have made many local people sick.

8 | Writing

Find out about a city in your country that is making great efforts to be more sustainable and write a report.

UNIT 3

ENERGY

Unit Goals

In this unit, you will find out about:

- various sources of energy
- their advantages and disadvantages
- nuclear waste and one country's approach

1 | Talking about the Topic

A Discuss the following questions with a partner or in a small group.

- When you are at home, how do you keep warm in winter?
- How do you keep cool in summer?
- Do you use gas or electricity when cooking? Why? Which is better for the environment?
- What other energy-consuming devices do you use at home?
- What could you do to reduce your energy consumption?

B Which of these resources can be used to produce heat or electricity? Circle your answers. Use a dictionary to check any words you don't know.

oil   gas   coal   wood   uranium   garbage   old tires   animal dung   sugar
rivers   wind   hot springs   waves   the sun   tide   hydrogen

C How harmful are they for the environment? Write V (very), L (a little) or N (not) next to the answers you have circled. Compare your answers with other students' answers.

2 | Words in Context

What do you think the words and phrases in bold type below mean? Try to guess, and then check them in a dictionary.

- ☐ Every car using gasoline or diesel **contributes to** the city's air pollution.
- ☐ The **nuclear** power station in Fukushima exploded after being struck by a tsunami.
- ☐ Nuclear waste is **radioactive**, and so it's extremely dangerous.
- ☐ The **temperature** inside a garbage incinerator can be as much as 1,000 degrees Celsius.
- ☐ Eating too much sugar can be **harmful** for your health.
- ☐ Do you **discard** your old textbooks at the end of the year, or do you keep them?
- ☐ Cigarettes contain many **substances** that can cause cancer and other diseases.
- ☐ Fuels made from plants and trees are called **biofuels**.
- ☐ Biofuels are **carbon-neutral** because they **absorb** carbon as they grow and **release** it when they're burned.
- ☐ Despite the problems it causes, coal is still a **major** energy source.

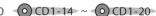

A Listen and take short notes. Then share your notes with a partner or in a small group.

Tip: When doing a listening and note-taking task on your own device, you may need to use the pause button. However, it is also useful when just listening. You can decide how often and how long to pause, and gradually reduce and shorten the pauses as you get more accustomed to listening. The eventual goal is to be able to understand lectures and take notes in real time.

- our main energy sources: _____
- problems: _____
- **nuclear energy**
  fuel used: _____
  a serious problem: _____
- **garbage**
  an advantage: _____
  a problem: _____
  a solution: _____
- **discarded tires**
  two ways they can be used: _____
  _____
  two problems: _____
  _____
- **animal dung**
  when it is a problem: _____
  when it is not: _____
- **gasohol**
  energy source: _____
  advantage: _____
  on the other hand: _____
- **seven cleaner energy sources**

  1 _____   5 _____
  2 _____   6 _____
  3 _____   7 _____
  4 _____

B Use your notes and your own words to present a short summary of what you have found out.

4 | Read and Share   Renewable Sources of Energy

Form a small group. Each member will choose one reading passage. Read yours carefully and be ready to answer questions about it. Then ask the other members the following questions about their reading passages. Finally, summarize what you have found out.

- Where does ... come from?
- How is it used?
- Can you give any examples?
- What are the advantages?
- What are the disadvantages?

ENERGY RESOURCES

Solar Energy	
source	
process	
examples	
advantages	
disadvantages	

Geothermal Energy	
source	
process	
examples	
advantages	
disadvantages	

Tidal Energy	
source	
process	
examples	
advantages	
disadvantages	

Wind Energy	
source	
process	
examples	
advantages	
disadvantages	

Hydrogen	
source	
process	
examples	
advantages	
disadvantages	

5 | Discussion

Discuss the following questions with a partner or in a small group.

- How could energy from solar power and wind be stored when it's not needed?
- What are some ways in which energy is wasted? (e.g. vending machines)
- What could you do or stop doing to save energy?
  (Consider air conditioners, washing machines, elevators, etc.)
- How do you feel about nuclear energy?
- What are its advantages and disadvantages?
- Should more nuclear power stations be built in Japan?

6 | Words in Context

What do you think the words and phrases in bold type below mean? Try to guess, and then check them in a dictionary.

☐ Careful driving helps **prevent** accidents.
☐ Solar energy isn't **available** at night.
☐ The main **objective** of this campaign is to save energy.
☐ The new nuclear **reactor** produces a lot of energy.
☐ This is where we **store** our solar panels before shipping them abroad.
☐ We have various sports **facilities**, including a soccer stadium and a pool.

7 | Listening   A Permanent Solution to a Serious Problem

🎧 DL 021~025   ⊙ CD1-21 ~ ⊙ CD1-25

A **Listen and take short notes. Then share your notes with a partner or in a small group.**

- how to stop global warming: _____
- a problem with solar power: _____
- a problem with hydroelectric power: _____
- a more reliable energy source: _____
- why not zero-carbon?: _____
- other advantages: _____
- its safety record: _____
- a serious issue: _____
- the usual approach: _____
- Onkalo: _____
- details of the facility: _____
- the final stage: _____

B **Use your notes and your own words to present a short summary of what you have found out.**

8 | Project   A More Sustainable Energy Plan

Your government's energy plan for the next ten years depends too much on energy from coal, gas and nuclear power. Work in a small group, discuss why the current plan should be changed, and prepare a proposal that would meet your country's entire energy needs with renewable energy. Include at least eight different sources of energy and five measures for reducing energy consumption.

Proposal

sources	·
	·
	·
	·
	·
	·
	·
	·
measures	·
	·
	·
	·
	·

9 | Vocabulary Review

Fill each space with a suitable word or phrase from this unit. You may need to change some words so that they fit grammatically.

1 When you cook rice, it .... a lot of water and becomes soft.

2 .... clothes can be turned into other useful products such as carpets.

3 High energy costs and bad management .... to the company's huge losses last year.

4 The strange black .... found on the seashore was actually a kind of seaweed.

5 The new laptops aren't .... yet, but we expect to have some next week.

6 One of the .... of our research is to develop new sources of energy that are both cheap and reliable.

7 In summer, we turn on the air conditioner when the .... exceeds 26 degrees.

8 The modern library is the most popular .... in this city.

9 He works for a .... bank, one of the biggest in Europe.

10 Plastic waste in the ocean is .... for turtles and fish.

10 | Writing

Find out about one of the following and write a report.

1 The advantages and disadvantages of nuclear energy

2 At least five ways to store energy from renewable sources such as sunshine and wind

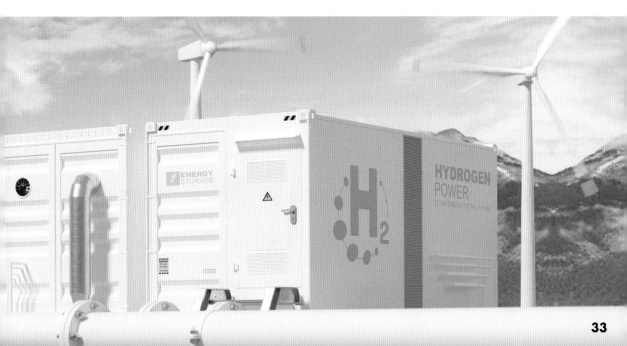

UNIT 4

CLIMATE CHANGE

Unit Goals

In this unit, you will find out about:

- causes of global warming
- consequences of global warming
- four ways to combat global warming

1 | Talking about the Topic

Discuss the following questions with a partner or in a small group.

- What causes global warming?
- Why is it a problem?
- What should be done about it?

2 | Words in Context

What do you think the words and phrases in bold type below mean? Try to guess, and then check them in a dictionary.

- ☐ I was **trapped** inside an elevator for almost two hours after it broke down.
- ☐ The rocket passed quickly through the **atmosphere** on its way to the moon.
- ☐ We need to stop burning **fossil fuels** such as gas, oil and coal.
- ☐ A scientist **predicted** global warming over 150 years ago.
- ☐ If we **reduce** the amount of energy we use, we can also save money.
- ☐ The bad harvest was **primarily** due to heavy rain, although there were other causes too.
- ☐ Farmers use **fertilizers** to increase the amount of food they can grow.
- ☐ I put **soil** into a planter and grew some tomatoes.

Listen and write your answers to the following questions. Then share your answers with a partner or in a small group.

Tip: It is important to recognize cause-effect relationships. Various words and phrases are used to show these.

a cause   an effect   a reason   a result   a consequence
because   so   for   as
due to   owing to   on account of   caused by
This is because   Because of this

1 When did global warming start?

_____

2 What is causing it?

_____

3 What will happen if we don't cut these emissions?

_____

4 What are the three greenhouse gases caused by humans?

_____

5 Which has the biggest impact?

_____

6 Where does it come from?

_____

7 What are the main sources of methane emissions?

_____

8 What causes nitrous oxide emissions?

_____

9 Why is it important to protect forests?

_____

10 What other carbon sink was mentioned?

_____

4 | Discussion

One approach to the problem of climate change is to reduce greenhouse gas emissions and restore sinks. This is called "mitigation." In Section 3 you have found out about the greenhouse gases and where they come from.

- What can we do to reduce emissions of
  - carbon dioxide?
  - methane?
  - nitrous oxide?
- What can we do to increase carbon sinks?

5 | Words in Context

What do you think the words and phrases in bold type below mean? Try to guess, and then check them in a dictionary.

- ☐ It's very hot today. If you go jogging, you may experience **heat stroke**.
- ☐ The **frequency** of major storms has recently increased to over ten per year.
- ☐ After heavy rain, we have **floods**, and after a hot, dry summer, we have **droughts**.
- ☐ Fertilizers help to make fields more **fertile**.
- ☐ If they don't get enough to eat, people **suffer** from **malnutrition**.
- ☐ If people use an anti-bacterial drug too often, the bacteria may become **resistant** to it.
- ☐ For someone who grew up in Singapore, it's hard to **adapt** to the climate of Alaska.

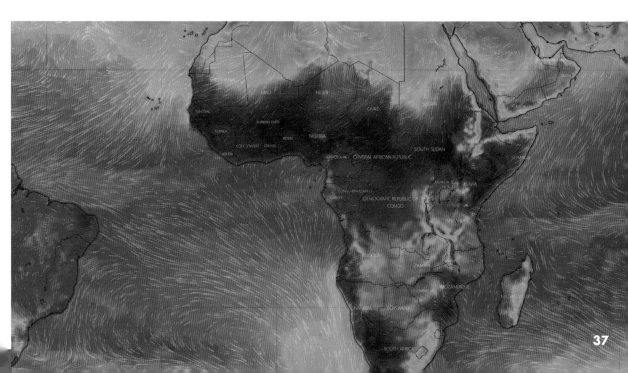

6 | Listening Consequences of Global Warming 🎧 DL 029~033 ⦿ CD1-29 ~ ⦿ CD1-33

Listen and take short notes. Then share your notes with a partner or in a small group.

- a seasonal threat to life: _____
- other threats to safety: _____
- threats to food security: _____
- threats to health: _____
- a problem affecting medical treatment: _____
- how sea levels are affected: _____
- causes of this: _____
- people and places most affected: _____
- problems affecting the Himalayan region: _____
- impacts on biodiversity: _____

Tip: Speakers often mention the sources of their information.

　　e.g. **Scientists predict that by the year 2100 ...**

　　　　According to researchers, up to one sixth of all species ...

A critical listener is more likely to take information seriously if it comes from scientists than from social network services.

7 | Discussion

You discussed mitigation in Section 4. Another approach to the problem of climate change is to deal with the consequences. This is called "adaptation" or "developing resilience."

- How can African farmers avoid heat stroke?
- How can coastal cities address the problem of rising sea levels?
- How can we ensure that the world has enough food for everyone despite climate change?
- How can we cope with infectious diseases and resistance to drugs?
- How can we save species that can't adapt to climate change? Is it necessary?

8 | Read and Share Climate Change: Some Solutions

Form a small group. Each member will choose one reading passage. Read yours carefully and be ready to present and explain it. The other members will listen and take notes without looking at the reading passages. After each presentation, they will report what they have found out. The presenter will add anything they overlooked and correct any misunderstandings.

Renewable Energy

Plant-based Diets

Planting Trees

CCS

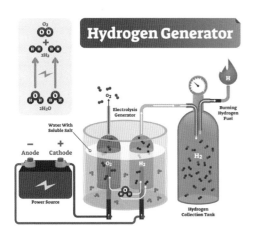

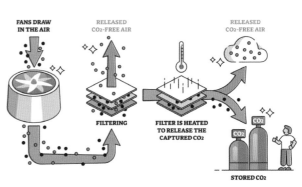

9 | Discussion

Discuss the following questions with a partner or in a small group.

- In what ways are you responsible for climate change?
- What could you do to reduce your own impact?
  Consider:
  - energy
  - transportation
  - shopping
  - food
  - trees
- Do you have any other ideas?

10 | Vocabulary Review

Fill each space with a suitable word or phrase from this unit. You may need to change some words so that they fit grammatically.

1 The only cure for severe .... is to provide people with enough food.

2 Because of the .... , people had to use boats instead of cars.

3 Nostradamus .... many terrible events, and some actually occurred.

4 There was a severe .... , and all the lakes and rivers became dry.

5 Researchers constantly measure the amount of greenhouse gases in the ....

6 The increase in the amount of rain each year is .... due to climate change.

7 Owing to the poor quality of the soil here, we need to use a lot of ....

8 After the traffic accident, she .... from severe headaches.

9 We must replace .... with renewable energy as soon as possible.

10 Some ski resorts have .... to the higher temperatures by using snowmaking machines.

11 | Writing

Find out about the most effective ways to cut greenhouse gas emissions according to Project Drawdown and write a report.

ENDANGERED SPECIES

Unit Goals

In this unit, you will find out about:

- endangered species
- why they are endangered
- efforts to protect them

1 | Talking about the Topic

Discuss the following questions with a partner or in a small group.

- The giant panda is an endangered species. What does that mean?
- Why should we care if pandas die out?
- Have you ever seen an endangered species? Where?
- What are the names of some endangered species in your country?
- Why are they endangered?
- What should be done to protect them?

2 | Words in Context

What do you think the words and phrases in bold type below mean? Try to guess, and then check them in a dictionary.

☐ **Biologists**, who research about living things, keep discovering new species.

☐ A researcher **identified** an unfamiliar animal as a species of bat.

☐ The Japanese wolf became **extinct**, which means we'll never have a chance to see one again.

☐ As a result of large-scale **logging**, very few trees remain in the area.

☐ Zoos can help increase the population of rare species by **breeding** them **in captivity**.

☐ Hunting is **illegal** in national parks, and there are severe penalties.

☐ The most serious **threat** to endangered species is the loss of **habitat**, their natural environment.

☐ The international trade in **ivory** was banned in order to save elephants, but **poachers** continue to kill them.

A　**Listen and take short notes. Then share your notes with a partner or in a small group.**

- the number of species identified: _____
- the number at risk: _____
- endemic species: _____

- **the giant panda**

  their natural habitat: _____

  the biggest threat: _____

  how their population recovered: _____

  the present number: _____

- **the vaquita**

  what they are: _____

  where they live: _____

  the present population: _____

  why they are endangered: _____

  measures to protect them: _____

- **the Iriomote wildcat**

  the main threats: _____

  measures to protect them: _____

- **two endemic bird species in New Zealand**

  their names: _____

  an unusual characteristic: _____

  the reason why they became endangered: _____

- **elephants**

  the main threat: _____

  some uses of ivory: _____

  a measure aimed at protecting elephants: _____

- **the Asiatic lion**

  location: _____

  population: _____

  a surprising fact: _____

B Use your notes and your own words to present a short summary of what you have found out.

4 | Discussion

One way to save endangered species is to capture them and keep them in zoos. Try to think of at least three advantages and three disadvantages of this approach.

Things you might consider:
- benefits for the animals
- demerits for the animals
- benefits for conservation
- potential management crises

Further questions
- What is the difference between a zoo and a safari park?
- Which would you rather work in? Why?

Tip: When presenting both advantages and disadvantages, you may want to use a transition phrase such as *on the other hand*.

Form a small group. Each member will choose one reading passage. Read yours carefully and be ready to answer questions about it. Then ask the other members the following questions about their reading passages. Finally, summarize what you have found out.

- Which species did you read about?
- Where do they live?
- How many are there?
- Why are they endangered?
- What has been done to protect them?

Black Rhinoceros

California Condor

Polar Bear

Mountain Gorilla

Lear's Macaw

A Work with a partner or in a small group. In this unit, you have found out why various species are endangered. List the reasons here.

- _____
- _____
- _____
- _____
- _____

Can you think of any other reasons why species become endangered?

- _____
- _____
- _____

B You have also found out about some ways to protect endangered species. List the approaches here.

- _____
- _____
- _____
- _____
- _____

Can you think of any more ways to protect endangered species?

- _____
- _____
- _____

7 | Role Play   Funding a Wildlife Park

Form a small group. You are at a meeting of the management committee for a wildlife park in a poor country. The government has cut your budget and you need to find other ways to pay for your staff and for compensation to farmers for damage caused by wild animals. How could you raise money to cover all your expenses?

First, discuss your own ideas.
Next, your teacher will present some more ideas. Listen and take notes.
Then choose which ideas you think would be the most useful.

8 | Vocabulary Review

Fill each space with a suitable word or phrase from this unit. You may need to change some words so that they fit grammatically.

1 If .... wasn't so valuable, people wouldn't kill elephants.

2 Thousands of species have become .... since the beginning of the 20th Century and no longer exist.

3 It's .... to hunt wild animals without a license.

4 Poor people can earn money from ...., but if it's allowed to continue, soon there will be no trees left.

5 Wild animals should be seen in their natural ...., not in zoos.

6 A famous .... will give a talk about wild plants in the Himalayas next week.

7 The greatest .... to the polar bear is climate change.

8 She knows a lot about butterflies, and she can .... over 250 different species.

9 Two .... were arrested after shooting a rhinoceros in the national park.

10 A Japanese researcher has been able to .... tuna in ....

9 | Writing

Find out about an endangered species not mentioned in this unit and write a report.

UNIT 6

TROPICAL RAINFORESTS

Unit Goals

In this unit, you will find out about:

- the importance of tropical rainforests
- the main threats to tropical rainforests
- four ways to save tropical rainforests

1 | Talking about the Topic

Discuss the following questions with a partner or in a small group.

- In which parts of the world can we see tropical rainforests?
- What are some products we get from tropical rainforests?
- What do you know about the people who live there?
- Why are tropical rainforests important for our planet?

2 | Words in Context

What do you think the words and phrases in bold type below mean? Try to guess, and then check them in a dictionary.

Tip: We can often guess the meaning of a word from examples provided.

    e.g. They cultivate **crops** such as corn, potatoes and beans.

- ☐ Oceans **occupy** about two thirds of the Earth's surface.
- ☐ Costa Rica has amazing **biodiversity**. For example, there are over 1,250 different species of butterfly.
- ☐ We can learn a lot from **indigenous** cultures like that of the Maori.
- ☐ The **preservation** of the rainforests is essential for maintaining biodiversity.
- ☐ What are the main **factors** that are responsible for rainforest destruction?
- ☐ The **construction** of highways through the Amazon is a major threat to the rainforest.
- ☐ Agriculture has a **substantial** impact on the environment.
- ☐ The new **settlement** already has more than 400 homes.
- ☐ It took many years, but **eventually** the new dam was finished.
- ☐ Even though one plant seems to **resemble** another, their flowers are a little different.

3 | Listening The Importance of Tropical Rainforests

DL 042~045 CD1-42 ~ CD1-45

Listen and write your answers to the following questions. Then share your answers with a partner or in a small group.

1 Where are the tropical rainforests located?

_____

2 What products do we get from them?

_____

3 What kinds of people live there?

_____

4 Why are tropical rainforests important for us?

_____

4 | Listening The Threats to Tropical Rainforests

DL 046~047 CD1-46 ~ CD1-47

A Listen and take short notes. Then share your notes with a partner or in a small group.

Tip: Short talks sometimes include helpful organizational cues.

e.g. There are **six reasons** for this.

● the threats

1 _____

_____

2 _____

_____

3 _____

_____

4 _____

_____

5 _____

_____

6 _____

_____

B Use your notes and your own words to present a short summary of what you have found out.

5 | Read and Share Four Ways to Save the Rainforests

Form a small group. Each member will choose one reading passage. Read yours carefully and be ready to present and explain it. The other members will listen and take notes without looking at the reading passages. After each presentation, they will report what they have found out. The presenter will add anything they overlooked and correct any misunderstandings.

Tip: How to make sure your listeners are following your presentation:

OK? Did you follow that? Would you like me to say that again?

Ecosystem services? Those are the benefits we get from rainforests, like clean water and hydroelectric power.

Payment for Ecosystem Services

Ecotourism

Carbon Offsets

Debt-for-Nature Agreements

Work with a partner or in a small group to complete this outline.

Rainforest products

Other reasons why rainforests are important

- _____
- _____
- _____

The main threats

- _____
- _____
- _____
- _____
- _____
- _____

Successful Approaches
- Costa Rica #1

- Costa Rica #2

- Brazil

- Bolivia

---

7 | Discussion

Discuss the following questions with a partner or in a small group.

- Consider the reasons why rainforests are being destroyed. Are we, as consumers, responsible for this in any way?
- How could we contribute to protecting the rainforests or, better still, increasing them?
- What could our own governments do to help protect and increase tropical rainforests?

8 | Vocabulary Review

Fill each space with a suitable word or phrase from this unit. You may need to change some words so that they fit grammatically.

1 One common .... involved in rainforest destruction almost everywhere is agriculture.

2 The rainforests are inhabited by .... people.

3 The members of different Amazon communities .... each other, but speak different languages.

4 Japanese .... companies use a lot of imported wood in order to build houses.

5 The Amazon has great .... : almost half of the world's species live there.

6 It's a good plan, as the cost is low and the benefits are ....

7 Each rainforest tree is .... by hundreds of different species.

8 There are no large towns, just a few small .... beside the river.

9 The forest was badly damaged by the fires, but .... , after several years, the trees started to grow again.

10 Policies concerning rainforests should focus on .... rather than development.

9 | Writing

Find out about the Roundtable on Sustainable Palm Oil, its objectives and why it is controversial, and write a report.

UNIT 7

TOURISM

Unit Goals

In this unit, you will find out about:
- ecotourism and its impact on the environment
- responsible tourism
- four community tourism projects

1 | Talking about the Topic

Discuss the following questions with a partner or in a small group.

- Which country would you most like to visit? Why?
- What are the most important factors for you in choosing a holiday destination? (cost, climate, safety, etc.)
- What are the main attractions for foreign tourists in your country?
- What problems might foreign tourists experience in your country?
- What kinds of jobs are available in the tourism industry?
- Would you like to do any of these jobs?

2 | Words in Context

What do you think the words and phrases in bold type below mean? Try to guess, and then check them in a dictionary.

- ☐ Water and food are both **vital** for life.
- ☐ The World Food Program **alleviates** hunger by providing free school meals.
- ☐ The plane will reach its **destination** in about eleven hours' time.
- ☐ Car **manufacturers** are increasing their production of electric cars.
- ☐ Some people **offset** their carbon emissions by planting trees.
- ☐ The new 50% tax on plane tickets is **controversial**; some people support it, but others are very angry about it.
- ☐ It's **fraudulent** to sell someone a fake diamond pretending that it's real.
- ☐ The island is so **remote** that it takes two weeks to get there by ship.
- ☐ We have only two **options**: regular fare or first class.

3 | Listening Sustainable Tourism

Listen and write your answers to the following questions. Then share your answers with a partner or in a small group.

1 Why is the tourism industry important?

_____

2 What was probably the first ecotourism destination?

_____

3 Why should Europeans avoid faraway ecotourism destinations like Costa Rica?

_____

4 Why should tourists avoid traveling by plane?

_____

5 Why might it become impossible to visit the Maldives Islands?

_____

6 What are some ways to make flying more sustainable?

_____

7 Why are carbon offsets controversial?

_____

8 In which country can we enjoy zero-emission train journeys?

_____

9 What is the cheapest way to visit Santa Claus in his hometown without harming the environment on the way?

_____

_____

4 | Discussion

Discuss the following questions with a partner or in a small group.

- What are the benefits of traveling abroad for tourists?
- In what ways could tourism benefit the local community?
- What are some problems tourism might cause for the local community?
- What advice would you give foreign tourists when visiting your country in order to avoid causing problems?

5 | Words in Context

What do you think the words and phrases in bold type below mean? Try to guess, and then check them in a dictionary.

☐ Visitors to the Great Barrier Reef want to see the **coral** and the fish.

☐ Every year, turtles **migrate** to this island from over a thousand kilometers away.

☐ There's a **shortage** of water now, so be careful not to waste it.

☐ This is a **casual** event, so it doesn't matter what you wear.

☐ We were impressed with the **attitude** of the staff. They were very polite.

☐ I respect all of my teachers, but I especially **look up to** my history professor.

☐ The official building **code** has been revised, and many poorly-built tourist hotels will have to be rebuilt.

☐ This country is ruled by a **dictator**. Nobody dares to challenge him.

6 | Listening   Responsible Tourism   🎧 DL 056   ⊚ CD 1-56

A **Listen and take short notes. Then share your notes with a partner or in a small group.**

Problems caused by tourism
1 problem: _____
example: _____
2 problem: _____
example: _____
3 problem: _____
example: _____
4 problem: _____
example: _____
A responsible tourism code
1 Respect _____
example: _____
2 Respect _____
example: _____
3 Respect _____
example: _____
4 Respect _____
example: _____

B **Use your notes and your own words to present a short summary of what you have found out.**

Form a small group. Each member will choose one reading passage. Read yours carefully and be ready to answer questions about it. Then ask the other members the following questions about their reading passages. Finally, summarize what you have found out.

- Where is this project?
- Who initiated it?
- What are its goals?
- What special features does it have?
- What are the benefits for the local community?

Runa Tupari

Tumani Tenda

REST

Chalalan Ecolodge

8 | Role Play A New Resort

A large company called Three Oceans Resorts is planning to build a tourist resort on a beautiful island in the Philippines. The project will include a convention center, a luxury hotel, a casino, golf courses and a yacht marina. In order to avoid conflict with the local residents, the company needs to persuade them of the benefits the project will bring for the local community. They will also need to address any concerns about environmental and social impacts.

Students will be divided into three teams: Team A, B and C.

Team A: representatives of Three Oceans Resorts

Your task is to think of all the ways that your project will benefit the community and all the ways that you could minimize its environmental impact. This will be good for your international image. But remember, as a business, you have to be profitable. If you build the resort and it later fails, nobody will benefit.

Team B: representatives of the local community

Your task is to think of all the ways the project could harm your community and all the things you want them to do in order to gain your approval. Note: you will only oppose the project if your reasonable requests are rejected or if you don't trust the company to keep its promises.

Team C: environment experts

Your task is to think of all the potential environmental impacts of the project and advise the other two groups about how the impacts could be mitigated or avoided. Note that if environmental impacts are not fully addressed, both the company and the community will be badly affected.

There are further instructions on the next page.

Stage 1

Each team will brainstorm for ideas. Try to do this in English. Take notes of all ideas.

▼

Stage 2

Students will form new groups, each consisting of at least one member from each team. The aim of stage 2 is not to resist the project but to reach a successful conclusion that satisfies all three groups.

In each group, a member of Team A will give a short presentation to promote the project. The other members may interrupt (politely!) with questions or objections.

Sorry to interrupt, but ...

After the Team A representative has finished, the member of Team B will present any objections. Be sure to acknowledge the concessions already made by the Team A member.

I'm glad to know that you're willing to ... but I have some other concerns.

Then it is the turn of the Team C member.

Several environmental impacts have already been mentioned.
With regard to (impact one) I would like to suggest ...
There are several other impacts that we should consider ...

▼

Stage 3

Students will return to their stage 1 groups and report their results.

9 | Vocabulary Review

Fill each space with a suitable word or phrase from this unit. You may need to change some words so that they fit grammatically.

1 The airline .... its carbon emissions by donating solar panels to schools in Africa.

2 The most popular tourist .... last summer was Paris.

3 If you have a positive .... , you have a better chance of success.

4 I believe you all have very strong opinions on this very .... subject.

5 The doctor gave the injured tourist some medicine to .... the pain.

6 A good safety record and efficient online booking are .... for a successful airline.

7 She prefers to have a .... relationship with her students, so she uses their first names.

8 People from rural areas often .... to big cities to work in the tourism industry.

9 There's a .... of fresh vegetables now, so I have to buy frozen ones.

10 My mom started her own tourism company. I really .... her.

10 | Writing

Find out about one of the following and write a report.

1 Overtourism and measures to deal with it

2 How the Galapagos Islands have successfully coped with large numbers of tourists with very little environmental damage

UNIT 8

DEVELOPING COUNTRIES

Unit Goals

In this unit, you will find out about:
- how to decide if a country is developing
- five typical problems of developing countries
- the causes of these problems
- ways to solve these problems
- fair trade

1 | Talking about the Topic

Discuss the following questions with a partner or in a small group.

- What countries do you think of when you hear the term 'developing countries'?
- What is the usual standard by which the level of development is measured?
- What is the meaning of sustainable development?
- What are the Sustainable Development Goals?
- Why are some countries wealthier than others?
- In what ways does your country help less developed countries?

2 | Words in Context

What do you think the words and phrases in bold type below mean? Try to guess, and then check them in a dictionary.

- ☐ London and Tokyo have many things **in common**, but there are also many differences.
- ☐ The **life expectancy** of Japanese women is the longest in the world.
- ☐ It's **misleading** to say that Japan is a safe country, as there are many earthquakes.
- ☐ He studied in New York, so I **assume** he can speak English.
- ☐ I have a few **debts**, but I hope to pay the money back soon.
- ☐ The economic growth rate is a good **indicator** of the strength of the economy.
- ☐ The government is **committed** to providing free school meals for all children.
- ☐ My uncle is very **generous**; he regularly donates money to the local food bank.
- ☐ There are areas of **poverty** even in rich countries.

A Listen and write your answers to the following questions. Then share your answers with a partner or in a small group.

1 How does the IMF decide whether or not a nation is a developing country?

_____

2 How can we measure a country's living standards?

_____

3 What does the Gini Index tell us?

_____

4 What unique measure was adopted in Bhutan?

_____

5 What are some high-tech products made in developing countries?

_____

6 How do we know debt is a misleading indicator of wealth?

_____

7 How much of their wealth have rich countries promised to share with poor countries?

_____

8 How much did they spend on ODA in 2022?

_____

B Present a short summary of what you have found out.

4 | Brainstorming   Problems, Causes and Solutions

Here are some problems that exist in many developing countries. Form a small group and discuss some possible causes and potential solutions. Take notes of your group's main ideas.

Hunger	
causes	
solutions	

Disease	
causes	
solutions	

Illiteracy	
causes	
solutions	

Unemployment	
causes	
solutions	

Homelessness	
causes	
solutions	

5 | Read and Share Problems and Solutions

Form a small group. Each member will choose one reading passage. Read yours carefully and be ready to answer questions about it. Then ask the other members the following questions about their reading passages. Finally, summarize what you have found out.

- What are the main causes of ... in developing countries?
- What are some possible solutions?

Research Form

Hunger	
causes	
solutions	

Disease	
causes	
solutions	

Illiteracy	
causes	
solutions	

Unemployment	
causes	
solutions	

Homelessness	
causes	
solutions	

6 | Consolidation

Work with a partner or in a small group. In Sections 4 and 5, you have discussed the causes of five different problems and potential solutions. Close your book, take a sheet of paper and write the five problems. Then try to write as many causes and solutions as you can remember for each problem.

7 | Words in Context

What do you think the words and phrases in bold type below mean? Try to guess, and then check them in a dictionary.

☐ How can anyone **confirm** that the farmers were paid a fair price for their coffee?
☐ The label **certifies** that this is a fair trade product.
☐ The **cooperative** helps its members to sell their products.
☐ Companies **exploit** their workers through low wages and poor conditions.
☐ The workers' union **negotiated** with the company to get higher wages.
☐ Your idea has great **potential**. Let's try it and see if it works as well as we expect.

A Listen and take short notes. Then share your notes with a partner or in a small group

- top five coffee-producing countries: _____
- an unfair situation: _____
- an attempt to fix the problem: _____
- a matter of trust: _____
- the solution: _____
- about the farmers & workers

1 _____

2 _____

3 _____

4 _____

- extra benefits: _____
- a misunderstanding: _____
- another problem: _____

Counter Culture: _____
- an advantage of direct trade: _____
- a disadvantage of direct trade: _____

The Divine Chocolate Company: _____
- a unique feature: _____
- an advantage for farmers: _____

The Madagascar Chocolate Company: _____
- factory location: _____
- a major advantage for Madagascar: _____

- a potentially better approach: _____
- a counter-argument: _____
- a key element of fair trade: _____

B Use your notes and your own words to present a short summary of what you have found out.

Tips:

1 Speakers often use the words *this* and *that* when referring to what they have just said.

Listen again to what the speaker said about the Madagascar Chocolate Company.

That*'s what the Madagascar Chocolate Company does.*

What does it do?

Listen again to the final part, where the speaker talks about charity.

*But how many coffee drinkers would be **willing to do that**?*

Willing to do *what*?

2 Does the speaker expect an answer to this question? No. This is called a rhetorical question.

You can often recognize such questions by a falling intonation at the end.

9 | Discussion

Discuss the following questions with a partner or in a small group.

> You have just listened to a talk about fair trade related to coffee and chocolate.
> * What other products are sold with the Fairtrade label? Are they expensive? If so, do you mind paying more?
> * Which approach is best in your opinion: fair trade, direct trade, The Divine Chocolate Company's approach or The Madagascar Chocolate Company's approach? Why?

10 | Vocabulary Review

Fill each space with a suitable word or phrase from this unit. You may need to change some words so that they fit grammatically.

1 I wouldn't want to work for a company that .... its workers.

2 This new drug has the .... to save many lives.

3 My friend has donated thousands of dollars to charity. She's very ....

4 Indians don't live as long as Japanese. In other words, their .... is shorter.

5 I borrowed a lot of money, so now I have a big ....

6 The rice farmers' .... has its own bank and labor union.

7 My wife and I have a lot in .... For example, we both support fair trade.

8 Can you .... that there are no children working on this farm?

9 If you .... with the shopkeeper, you might get a lower price.

10 It's .... to say a farm product is fairly traded when there are no benefits for the farmer.

11 | Writing

Find out about one of the following and write a report.

1 Why some countries are much poorer than others

2 An organization or project that supports sustainable development in poor countries

UNIT 9

PEACE AND CONFLICT

Unit Goals

In this unit, you will find out about:

- the Nobel Peace Prize
- people and organizations that were awarded the prize
- ways to resolve disputes peacefully

1 | Talking about the Topic

Discuss the following questions with a partner or in a small group.

- When do you feel most at peace? (e.g. When I'm sleeping.)
- What events could disturb your peace? (e.g. An earthquake.)
- You live in a peaceful country, but many of your fellow citizens don't feel peace in their lives. What kinds of problems do they have?
  - children:
  - young adults:
  - elderly people:

- The country you live in is rich. How can your government help bring peace to people in poorer parts of the world with the following problems?
  - people who can afford only one meal a day
  - people made homeless due to civil war
  - people living under a brutal dictatorship
  - people whose island nation will soon be covered by the sea
  - people with treatable illnesses who cannot afford medicine
  - children who have to work all day in mines or on cocoa plantations

2 | Words in Context

What do you think the words and phrases in bold type below mean? Try to guess, and then check them in a dictionary.

- ☐ Before he died, he prepared a **will** in which he asked for all of his money to be given to his favorite charity.
- ☐ He quit drinking alcohol **for the sake of** his health.
- ☐ I don't **regret** quitting my job; I think it was a very good decision.
- ☐ She **established** a charity to support homeless people.
- ☐ The prize was **awarded** to someone who led a campaign for peace.
- ☐ The **committee** that makes the decisions **consists of** five experts.
- ☐ Each **individual** student received a graduation **diploma**.
- ☐ After the death of the dictator, political freedom was **restored**.
- ☐ The president is very **autocratic**: anyone who **resists** him is arrested by the police.

3 | Listening   The Nobel Peace Prize

DL 073~076   CD2-18 ~ CD2-21

A Listen and take short notes. Then share your notes with a partner or in a small group.

- how Nobel became rich: _____
- his will: _____
- his probable reason: _____
- the five awards: _____
- winners of the first Nobel Peace Prize: _____
  _____
- the sixth award: _____
- what the winners of the Peace Prize receive: _____
- when the winners are announced: _____
- who chooses the winners: _____
- who can receive the award: _____
- the winner in 2012: _____
- examples of winners not directly involved in peacekeeping:

2004: _____
2005: _____
2006: _____
2007: _____
2020: _____
2021: _____
2022: _____
2023: _____

B Use your notes and your own words to present a short summary of what you have found out.

4 | Discussion

Discuss the following questions with a partner or in a small group.

- Why do you think the EU was awarded the Nobel Peace Prize?
- How do you feel about this choice?
- In what way were the achievements of the 2004-2007 winners related to peace?
- Which person from your country was awarded the Nobel Peace Prize?
- How do you feel about that choice?

5 | Read and Share   Peacemakers

Form a small group. Each member will choose one reading passage. Read yours carefully and be ready to present and explain it. The other members will listen and take notes without looking at the reading passages. After each presentation, they will report what they have found out. The presenter will add anything they overlooked and correct any misunderstandings.

ICAN: the International Campaign to Abolish Nuclear Weapons

WFP: the World Food Program

MSF: Médecines Sans Frontières

ICBL: the International Campaign to Ban Landmines

6 | Project   The Global Peace Fund

When the Cold War ended between the US and the Soviet Union, many people were expecting a "peace dividend", with a lot of money being diverted from military spending to economic development. They were disappointed. Military expenditure continued to grow, and by 2022 it had reached $2,24 trillion a year. The arms race is not only wasteful; it is also dangerous. Imagine that all countries agreed to reduce their arms spending by one third. There would still be more than enough for defense, but over $700 billion would be available for making the world a better place. That is the Global Peace Fund. It doesn't exist, but it could and should.

How could the money be spent? Form a group and share your ideas. List at least 10 proposals, e.g., to fight climate change.

- _____
- _____
- _____
- _____
- _____
- _____
- _____
- _____
- _____
- _____

7 | Brainstorming Resolving a Dispute

Country A and country B are neighbors on the same island. They have never agreed about where the border should be between them, but now there is a risk of war. How could the dispute be resolved peacefully? Form a small group and try to think of at least 10 solutions. Feel free to be creative!

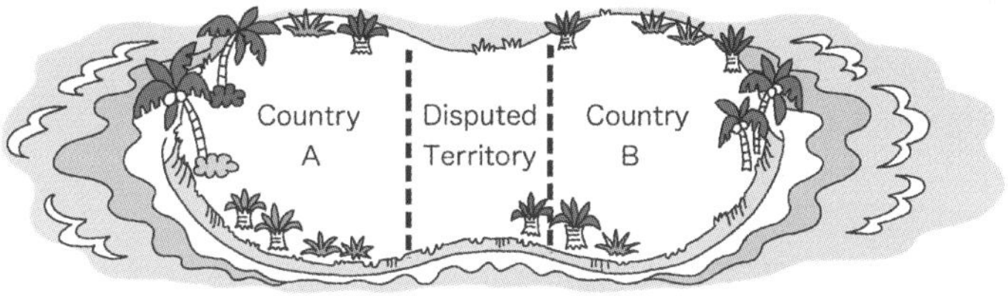

- _____
- _____
- _____
- _____
- _____
- _____
- _____
- _____
- _____
- _____

What do you think the words and phrases in bold type below mean? Try to guess, and then check them in a dictionary.

- ☐ Three political parties formed an **alliance** in order to win the election.
- ☐ Two countries had a political disagreement, but the **dispute** was **resolved** peacefully.
- ☐ A **territorial** dispute involves a disagreement about which country an area belongs to.
- ☐ **Institutions** such as the United Nations can help resolve disputes.
- ☐ The two nations negotiated and **ended up** with a fair agreement.
- ☐ For a country with no access to the sea, buying warships isn't **logical**.
- ☐ When a large **majority** of people don't support the government, it should quit.

9 | Listening Peaceful Solutions

DL 077~082   CD2-22 ~ CD2-27

A Listen and take short notes. Then share your notes with a partner or in a small group.

negotiation and compromise
- example: _____
- the result: _____

mediation
- example: _____

arbitration
- example: _____
- the result: _____

asking the people who live there
- examples: _____
- the results: _____

taking turns
- example: _____
- the agreement: _____

exchange of territory
- example: _____
- the cause of the problem: _____
- the solution: _____

B Use your notes and your own words to present a short summary of what you have found out.

10 | Discussion

Japan has some territorial disputes with neighboring countries. Consider each of the approaches you have just discussed in Sections 7 and 9 and propose solutions to the following disputes.

with Russia	
details of the dispute	
your proposals	

with South Korea	
details of the dispute	
your proposals	

with China	
details of the dispute	
your proposals	

11 | Further Discussion

Discuss the following questions with a partner or in a small group.

- The US maintains a number of military bases in Japan. In what ways do they benefit the US? How do they benefit Japan? Who pays for them?
- Some nations that have no enemies require their citizens to do military service for a year or more. Why? Should Japan consider introducing military service too?
- Fifteen nations are known to possess nuclear weapons. Which nations? Why?
- Japan has "three non-nuclear principles". What are they? Do you support them?

12 | Vocabulary Review

Fill each space with a suitable word or phrase from this unit. You may need to change some words so that they fit grammatically.

1 According to the instructions in her ...., all of her money was to be given to charity when she died.

2 Most Japanese would .... any proposal to develop or store nuclear weapons in their country.

3 This year, the government .... significant amounts of money to medical researchers.

4 A .... was formed to decide how the money should be used.

5 After long and unsuccessful negotiations, the two countries .... asking the UN to mediate their dispute.

6 The disagreement between the two states was .... peacefully.

7 Japan .... four main islands and many smaller ones.

8 Einstein .... having contributed to the development of the atomic bomb.

9 The United Nations was .... in 1945 and has worked hard to promote peace and prosperity.

10 The .... of countries in Europe belong to the European Union.

13 | Writing

Find out about a territorial dispute involving your country (or any other), the arguments on both sides, and potential solutions, and write a report.

UNIT 10

REFUGEES AND MIGRANTS

Unit Goals

In this unit, you will find out about:
- migrants, refugees and displaced persons
- true stories of migrants and refugees
- climate refugees

1 | Talking about the Topic

Discuss the following questions with a partner or in a small group.

- Why do many people move to a foreign country?
- What kinds of problems do they experience?
- Should foreigners be allowed to work?

2 | Words in Context

What do you think the words and phrases in bold type below mean? Try to guess, and then check them in a dictionary.

☐ My driver's license is about to **expire**. I need to apply for a new one.

☐ My employment **contract** shows how much I will be paid each month.

☐ It's sometimes difficult to **distinguish** between immigrants and tourists.

☐ **Persecution** is what happens to people who are attacked because of their religion or skin color.

☐ Is this visa **genuine**? It looks like a copy.

☐ Many **immigrants** come to the US from Latin America.

☐ Migrants without passports and visas are usually **detained** for a few weeks and then sent home.

☐ Many people were **displaced** by the floods and couldn't return to their homes for months.

☐ They had to **abandon** their homes after the town was destroyed by an earthquake.

☐ All the money in the NGO's **budget** was spent on feeding poor people.

DL 083~087   CD2-28 ~ CD2-32

A Listen and write your answers to the following questions. Then share your answers with a partner or in a small group.

1 Who do we call economic migrants?

_____

2 What kind of work do they do?

_____

3 How do they find work?

_____

4 How does this benefit their own countries?

_____

5 In what ways do legal migrants differ from those who enter and stay illegally?

_____

6 How do those hoping to enter illegally reach Europe?

_____

7 What has the EU done about this problem?

_____

8 In what way are refugees different from economic migrants?

_____

9 Why are they treated in this way?

_____

10 What may happen to them if they are sent home?

_____

11 Who are internally displaced people?

_____

12 Where do they live?

_____

13 How much money did the UNHCR have for their work in 2022?

_____

14 Why was that probably not enough?

_____

15 What is making the work of the UNHCR even harder?

_____

16 What did the World Bank report predict?

_____

17 What does the speaker predict?

_____

B **Present a short summary of what you have found out.**

4 | Discussion

Discuss the following questions with a partner or in a small group.

- In 2021, there were 1,255,694 refugees living in Germany but only 1,132 in Japan. Why is Japan so reluctant to accept refugees?
- On the other hand, Japan supports refugees in other ways. Can you think of some examples?
- What kinds of problems do refugees face after arriving in Japan?
- What kinds of support should they be given?
- What rights should refugees have?
  e.g. work
- In what ways can refugees contribute to the host country?
- Do you think the Japanese government should make it easier for refugees to come to Japan?

5 | Read and Share True Stories

Form a small group. Each member will choose one reading passage. Read yours carefully and be ready to present and explain it. The other members will listen and take notes without looking at the reading passages. After each presentation, they will report what they have found out. The presenter will add anything they overlooked and correct any misunderstandings.

A Refugee Weightlifter

Refugee Musicians

Refugee Farmers

A Climate Refugee?

---

6 | Words in Context

What do you think the words and phrases in bold type below mean? Try to guess, and then check them in a dictionary.

- ☐ In Amsterdam, some people live in houses that **float** on the water, so they aren't affected by floods.
- ☐ The judge **declared** that the prisoner must be released because he had committed no crime.
- ☐ Climate change is the most serious **issue** facing the world today.
- ☐ Many people feel that migrants who arrive illegally should be **deported** to where they came from.
- ☐ They volunteered to **host** a refugee family in their home.
- ☐ Foreign fishing boats aren't allowed to operate within our country's **Exclusive Economic Zone**.
- ☐ **In theory**, there's a clear distinction between genuine refugees and economic migrants, but in reality, it's often hard to tell the difference.

7 | Listening · Climate Refugees

 DL 088~092 · ⊚ CD2-33 ~ ⊚ CD2-37

A Listen and take short notes. Then share your notes with a partner or in a small group.

Kiribati

- the problem: _____
- the 3 choices: _____
  _____
  _____
- migration with dignity: _____
  _____
- an important statement: _____
  _____
- the case: _____
- New Zealand's program: _____
- the problem: _____
- how the UN could help: _____
- a surprising fact about Kiribati: _____
- how this could benefit the people in the future: _____
  _____
- the conditions for continued UN recognition: _____
- the ideal solution to the problem:
  _____

B Use your notes and your own words to present a short summary of what you have found out.

Tip: Notice how the speaker shows uncertainty about the future by using these words and phrases:

may	e.g. may be one of the first ... may get new homes ...
could	e.g. could be a reason ... could be solved ...
is likely to ...	e.g. is likely to continue ...

The Maldives is a nation in the Pacific Ocean consisting of a group of 1,192 islands with a total population of 550,000 people. The average height is about 1.5m above sea level. Because of rising sea levels caused by global warming, all of the islands will probably be uninhabitable by the year 2100. The people of the Maldives will need to find a new home.

Japan's share of historical greenhouse gas emitted since the Industrial Revolution is about 4%. Therefore, it has been suggested that Japan should provide a home for 4% of the population of Maldives. That would amount to 22,000 people. Japan has 14,125 islands (excluding the islands occupied by Russia), and 90% of them are uninhabited.

First, discuss whether or not Japan should accept this request, considering its responsibility for rising sea levels and its wealth compared to that of the Maldives.

If you approve, then prepare a basic plan on how to set up Maldives communities in the best locations, e.g. inhabited or uninhabited, remote or near to the mainland, necessary infrastructure, etc.

If you disapprove, then decide how you will help the Maldives to adapt to higher sea levels or compensate the people for the loss of their homeland.

Your decision	
Your reasons	
Your plan	

9 | Vocabulary Review

Fill each space with a suitable word or phrase from this unit. You may need to change some words so that they fit grammatically.

1   The doctor .... that the President had fully recovered from his medical problem.

2   This can't be a .... work permit. It has several spelling mistakes.

3   We need to sign a new rental .... for our apartment once a year.

4   I can't .... the original document from the photocopy.

5   Her grandparents were .... who moved to Hawaii from Japan in the 1920s and stayed.

6   He was .... from three different countries, and finally abandoned his ambition to live in Europe.

7   Our .... is only $650, so we can't afford to eat at expensive restaurants every day.

8   My passport has just ...., so I need to get a new one.

9   People who have experienced .... should be accepted as refugees.

10   ...., you need to book your flight in advance, but there are usually vacant seats on the day of the flight.

10 | Writing

Find out about one of the following and write a report.

1   The activities of an NGO that supports refugees in your country

2   The Refugee Olympic Team

3   The Refugee World Cup

THE UNITED NATIONS

Unit Goals

In this unit, you will find out about:
- the UN past and present
- the UN Security Council
- five UN agencies
- contrasting opinions about the UN

1 | Quiz What Do You Know about the United Nations?

A Discuss the following questions with a partner or in a small group.

1 When was the UN established? _____

2 How many countries belong to the UN? _____

3 Where is the headquarters of the UN? _____

4 Who is the current UN Secretary-General? _____

5 What happens at the UN General Assembly? _____

6 How many members does the UN Security Council have? _____

7 Which countries are the four biggest contributors to the UN regular budget?

_____ _____ _____ _____

8 What are the six official languages of the UN?

_____ _____ _____ _____ _____

9 What does the UN flag look like? _____

10 What does it symbolize? _____

B **Listen and check your answers to the Quiz.** DL 093~100   CD2-38 ~   CD2-45

C **Share your answers with a partner or in a small group.**

2 | Words in Context

What do you think the words and phrases in bold type below mean? Try to guess, and then
check them in a dictionary.

☐ The city was **devastated** by the earthquake.
☐ The union **represents** more than 25,000 firefighters.
☐ Many large companies have their **headquarters** in Tokyo.
☐ The government has various **agencies**, such as the Agency for Cultural Affairs.
☐ The president was **elected** again this year despite strong opposition to his policies.
☐ The **agenda** for today's committee meeting includes a vote on several new proposals.
☐ Several **resolutions** were proposed during the meeting, including one to hold all future
   meetings online.
☐ The UN cannnot mediate a dispute without the **approval** of the countries involved.
☐ The president has **vetoed** every proposal I made, so I'm not going to make any more.

3 | Listening The United Nations

A Listen again and take short notes. Then share your notes with a partner or in a small group.

- The League of Nations:
  _____

- The number of years served by the Secretary-General:
  _____

- A problem involving the UN Security Council:
  _____

- Nobel Peace Prizes:
  _____

- The way contributions from each country are decided:
  _____

B Use your notes and your own words to present a short summary of what you have found out.

4 | Discussion

Discuss the following questions with a partner or in a small group.

- In what ways might your country benefit from being a member of the UN?
- A survey by Pew Research in 2021 found that only 41% of Japanese have a positive image of the UN. Can you think of any reasons for this? How do you feel about the UN?
- As of 2021, only 1% of UN employees were Japanese. Why so few? Would you like to work for the UN? Why or why not?
- The UN is always short of money. Should there be a special UN tax? If so, who should pay?

5 | Read and Share Members of the UN Family

Form a small group. Each member will choose one reading passage. Read yours carefully and be ready to present and explain it. The other members will listen and take notes without looking at the reading passages. After each presentation, they will report what they have found out. The presenter will add anything they overlooked and correct any misunderstandings.

UNICEF

UNESCO

FAO

WHO

UNEP

6 | Words in Context

What do you think the words and phrases in bold type below mean? Try to guess, and then check them in a dictionary.

☐ Negotiating a peace agreement between the two countries was a great **accomplishment**.
☐ Using a water filter **makes sense**: it's much cheaper than buying bottled water.
☐ The minister was very **corrupt**. He transferred taxpayers' money to his private bank account.

7 | Listening 　Four Opinions about the United Nations

🎧 DL 101~104　　◉ CD2-46 ~ ◉ CD2-49

You will hear four opinions about the UN. Listen to each opinion twice.

A First, decide if it is favorable (F) or unfavorable (U).
　1 F or U 　　**2** F or U 　　**3** F or U 　　**4** F or U

B Next, decide if you agree (A) or disagree (D) with each opinion. Share your answers.
　1 A or D 　　**2** A or D 　　**3** A or D 　　**4** A or D

8 | Discussion

Discuss the following questions with a partner or in a small group.

● Japan pays about 8.5% of the UN budget. What benefits does Japan get?
● The following countries each have one vote in the UN General Assembly. How do you feel about this? Can you think of a fairer system?

population	size	share of UN budget
Japan: 125 million	Russia: 17 million square km	US: 22%
Nauru: 10,000	San Marino: 60 square km	Denmark: 0.5%

● The UN Security Council has five permanent members who can individually veto any UN resolution. Which countries are they? Why were they given this status?
● Should more countries become permanent members? If so, which? Why?
● Should the Security Council veto be abolished? Is this even possible?

9 | Discussion   The UN Calendar

A These are some important dates on the UN Calendar. What is the aim of each one? What could people do to celebrate them?

8 March	International Women's Day
31 May	World No Tobacco Day
5 June	World Environment Day
20 June	World Refugee Day
11 July	World Population Day
8 September	International Literacy Day
15 September	International Day of Democracy
21 September	International Day of Peace
16 October	World Food Day
24 October	United Nations Day
20 November	World Children's Day
10 December	Human Rights Day

B What special days would you like to add? Why?

(e.g. Should there be an Animal Rights Day?)

Visit the UN online list of International Days and Weeks. Choose an interesting Day, take notes and introduce it to your group.

e.g. English Language Day, World Bicycle Day, etc.

11 | Vocabulary Review

Fill each space with a suitable word or phrase from this unit. You may need to change some words so that they fit grammatically.

1 The .... of the FAO are in Rome.

2 The UN adopted a new .... to ban child labor.

3 Of all the WFP's .... , winning the Nobel Peace Prize was the greatest.

4 The flags around the UN building in New York .... 183 countries.

5 It .... to back up all your files in case your computer breaks down.

6 A new Secretary-General will be .... in a few years' time.

7 The UN has many different .... , including the UNHCR.

8 There are three items on our .... for today's meeting.

9 One member of the Security Council didn't .... of the proposal, so it failed.

10 I hope the US won't .... our plan to raise money for the UN by taxing the international arms trade.

12 | Writing

Find out about one of the following and write a report.

1 A member of the UN family not mentioned in Section 5

2 Proposals for reforming the UN Security Council and why they have not been successful so far

NATIONS UNIES

UNIT 12

HUMAN RIGHTS

Unit Goals

In this unit, you will find out about:

· the Universal Declaration of Human Rights
· the history of human rights
· human rights violations
· human rights campaigners

1 | Talking about the Topic

Discuss the following questions with a partner or in a small group.

- In your country, what human rights are guaranteed by law? List all of the ones you can think of.
- In which countries do people lack some of these rights? Which rights? Why?

2 | Listening   Some Basic Human Rights   DL 105   CD2-50

You will hear some of the rights that are listed in the Universal Declaration of Human Rights. Add any that are not on your list. Are they protected in your country? Are there any rights on your list that were not mentioned?

3 | Words in Context

What do you think the words and phrases in bold type below mean? Try to guess, and then check them in a dictionary.

- ☐ It's difficult for the police to **capture** dangerous criminals without harming them.
- ☐ **Given that** they knew who committed the crime, why did the police arrest someone else?
- ☐ Slavery was **abolished** in the US in 1865.
- ☐ The new law is **significant** because it recognizes animal rights for the first time.
- ☐ We're used to these rights, so we **take** them **for granted**.
- ☐ It was a good idea, but it was never **implemented**.
- ☐ The right to **vote** in free elections is a basic principle of **democracy**.
- ☐ Dictators don't **tolerate** opposition. Anyone who opposes them is sent to prison.
- ☐ The **current** government is more democratic than the previous one.

With your textbook closed, listen and take notes of the main points on a sheet of paper. Then open your textbook and try to answer the questions. Listen again and check your answers. Correct any mistakes and add any new answers. Then share your answers with a partner or in a small group.

1 Why is the Cyrus Cylinder so significant?

_____

2 What does the speaker think is appropriate?

_____

3 What examples of modern slavery does the speaker give?

_____

4 Why was the Magna Carta important?

_____

5 What does the speaker refer to as the "Magna Carta for the whole world"?

_____

6 How does the speaker feel about this?

_____

7 What is Article 21 about?

_____

8 How democratic is the world today?

_____

9 What did the Democracy Index report about the US?

_____

10 What shows that Article 24 is not fully implemented in Japan?

_____

5 | Discussion

A Here are some more controversial rights. In your opinion, which should be guaranteed by law?

People should / shouldn't have the right to ...
- silence
- breathe clean air
- marry someone of the same sex
- copy music and videos without paying
- have an abortion
- have water that is safe to drink
- ride a motorbike without a helmet
- drive while using a smartphone
- refuse a vaccination for a highly infectious disease

B Some rights are subject to age limitations.

From what age are you allowed to

drink alcohol? _____   smoke cigarettes? _____   drive a car? _____

get married? _____   vote? _____   work part-time? _____

get your own credit card? _____   gamble (including pachinko)? _____

rent an apartment _____

C Are these age limits appropriate?

HUMAN RIGHTS ARE MY PRIDE

AMNESTY
INTERNATIONAL

Form a small group. Each member will choose one reading passage. Read yours carefully and be ready to present and explain it. The other members will listen and take notes without looking at the reading passages. After each presentation, they will report what they have found out. The presenter will add anything they overlooked and correct any misunderstandings.

Martin Luther King Jr.

Peter Benenson

Craig Kielburger

Fashion Revolution

7 | Discussion

How do you feel about the following issues?

- animal rights
- support for homeless people
- providing economic aid to countries with authoritarian governments
- compulsory voting in elections (e.g. Australia)
- child labor
- the death penalty

8 | Vocabulary Review

Fill each space with a suitable word or phrase from this unit. You may need to change some words so that they fit grammatically.

1 It's no use having good policies if they aren't ....

2 The death penalty in the Netherlands was .... long ago.

3 If we take freedom .... we may lose it.

4 Which party did you .... for in the last election?

5 Many workers have lost their jobs, so there has been a .... increase in the number of homeless people.

6 In a .... , people can vote in free and fair elections every few years.

7 The new law on the right to privacy is .... being discussed and will be completed soon.

8 There was a lot of .... from car drivers to the ban on parking in the city center.

9 I was surprised that he accepted our request, ... he has refused so many times already.

10 The company manager doesn't .... carelessness. If workers make mistakes, they are fired.

9 | Writing

Find out about a human or animal rights problem in your country and write a report.

UNIT 13

GENDER ISSUES

Unit Goals

In this unit, you will find out about:
- the gender gap and why it exists
- ways to close the gap
- women who have helped make the world a better place

1 | Talking about the Topic

Discuss the following questions with a partner or in a small group.

In your country:

Life in general
- In what ways is life generally better for a woman?
- In what ways is it better for a man?

Stereotypes
- What kind of clothes, toys, hairstyles and hobbies are considered appropriate for girls? How about boys? Where do these ideas come from?

Education
- Is it better for girls and boys to study together, or in separate schools? Why?
- Are there any subjects that are studied only by girls or only by boys?

Jobs

- What kinds of jobs are mostly done by men? Why?
- How about jobs mostly done by women?
- Why do men tend to earn more than women, even when doing similar jobs?
- Why do so few women become top executives in major companies?

Marriage

- Should a woman quit her job after getting married?
- How about after having a baby? If so, for how long?
- Should all employers be required to pay for maternity leave?
- How about paternity leave?
- What household chores are women expected to do?
- What about men?

Politics

- When did Japanese women first get the right to vote?
- Why not until then?
- Why are there far more men than women in Japanese politics?

2 | Words in Context

What do you think the words and phrases in bold type below mean? Try to guess, and then check them in a dictionary.

- ☐ The law now bans **discrimination** against women in the workplace.
- ☐ The idea that women are weak at science **persists** despite the achievements of Marie Curie.
- ☐ She collects books by feminist writers, and has **accumulated** over 60 so far.
- ☐ The company I work for has a **flexible** working schedule, so I can start work at any time.
- ☐ The penalties for **non-compliance** with the Equal Pay Law have been increased.
- ☐ It's now **mandatory** for all buisinesses to report on their progress in eliminating gender-based discrimination in the workplace.
- ☐ A friend of mine took three months' **leave** from his job after his wife had a baby.
- ☐ According to the **quota**, at least 40% of new medical students must be female.
- ☐ The **minimum** legal wage is the same for women as for men, but women still earn less.
- ☐ One of our teachers has just quit, so we need to interview a few **candidates** for the job.

3 | Listening   Gender: Closing the Gap   🎧 DL 110~114   ⊙ CD2-55 ~ ⊙ CD2-59

With your textbook closed, listen and take notes of the main points on a sheet of paper. Then open your textbook and try to answer the questions. Listen again and check your answers. Correct any mistakes and add any new answers. Then share your answers with a partner or in a small group.

1 What does the World Economic Forum's annual report tell us about gender equality?

_____

2 What simple reason is often given for this problem?

_____

3 Why can we assume that is not the main reason in the case of the US?

_____

4 What are the main reasons for the pay gap?

- _____
- _____
- _____

5 Why is it important to close the gap?

- _____
- _____

6 How successful has Japan been in closing the gap?

_____

7 Which country is top of the WEF ranking?

_____

8 How did it achieve that status?

· _____

· _____

· _____

9 How much time can parents take off for childcare leave in Sweden?

_____

10 How can a quota system be used to give women a bigger role in politics?

_____

4 | Discussion

Discuss the following questions with a partner or in a small group.

- What do you think the Chinese proverb "women hold up half the sky" means?
- What should be done about the gender gap in Japan as regards wages?
- How does Japan's approach differ from that of Iceland?
- How likely is it that Japan will have a female prime minister within the next ten years? Why?
- What do you think of introducing a mandatory quota system for candidates?
- Would a candidate's gender influence your vote?

5 | Read and Share   Women Making the World a Better Place

A Form a small group. Each member will choose one reading passage. Read yours carefully and be ready to present and explain it. The other members will listen and take notes without looking at the reading passages. After each presentation, they will report what they have found out. The presenter will add anything they overlooked and correct any misunderstandings.

Maria Montessori

Malala Yousafzai

Marie Curie

Florence Nightingale

B Which of these four women do you admire most? Why? What other women do you know about who have helped make the world a better place? What did they do? If you could invite a famous Japanese woman to give a talk at your school or university, who would you invite?

6 | Discussion

A Do you agree or disagree with the following statements? Explain your reasons.

- Children's toys should be gender-free.
- School uniforms should be gender-free.
- School subjects should be gender-free.
- Boys are naturally better than girls at science and engineering.
- Girls should be encouraged to choose any career that attracts them.
- Hospitals should hire more female doctors and more male nurses.
- Female job applicants should be interviewed by female staff.
- When women have babies, they should quit work.

- Housework should be shared fairly between wives and husbands.
- All railway companies should provide women-only and men-only carriages on every train.
- If women want to have more influence in politics, they should vote for female candidates.
- Japan will never have a female prime minister.

B Discuss the following questions.

- What role should education play in promoting gender equality?
  (Consider elementary school, middle school, high school and university.)
- What are some other gender issues that concern you? Discuss each issue and potential solutions.

7 | Vocabulary Review

Fill each space with a suitable word or phrase from this unit. You may need to change some words so that they fit grammatically.

1 Establishing a .... for the proportion of female firefighters won't work if women don't want to fight fires.

2 It's .... for all supervisors to report any cases of sexual harassment.

3 All mothers should be able to take childcare .... after their child is born.

4 The .... legal age for marriage was changed, and is now 18 for both males and females.

5 Paying a man more than a woman for doing the same job is ....

6 Should the new employee be a woman, or are you .... about that?

7 Having been an engineer for over 30 years, she has .... a lot of experience.

8 We're proud of our .... with the latest gender equality laws.

9 The US wasn't the first country to allow women to vote, but this mistaken belief ....

10 Of the twenty .... who applied for the job, only one was a woman, but she did really well in the interview.

8 | Writing

Find out about one of the following and write a report.

1 A woman whose achievements you admire

2 A country that has made significant progress towards gender equality

UNIT 14

HEALTH AND LONGEVITY

Unit Goals

In this unit, you will find out about:
- life expectancy and longevity
- the Blue Zones
- ideas for solving problems related to Japan's aging society

1 | Talking about the Topic

Discuss the following questions with a partner or in a small group.

- Do you have a healthy diet?
- What healthy things do you eat and drink?
- How about unhealthy things?
- Do you get enough exercise?
- What kind of exercise do you do?
- How long do you sleep each night? Is it enough?
- Do you sometimes feel stress? What causes it?
- What can you do to relieve stress?
- What factors influence how long a person lives?
- Why do women generally live longer than men?

2 | Words in Context

What do you think the words and phrases in bold type below mean? Try to guess, and then check them in a dictionary.

☐ Apart from their hairstyles, the elderly twins looked **identical**.

☐ The average **lifespan** in Somalia is less than 60 years.

☐ The problem usually **associated with** coffee is difficulty sleeping.

☐ Eating too much and exercising too little often results in **obesity**.

☐ If you consume too much sugar in your diet, you may eventually suffer from **diabetes**.

☐ His long life is due to the **genes** he received from his parents.

☐ I **attribute** my good health to my vegetarian diet.

🎧 DL 115~119　◉ CD2-60　~　◉ CD2-64

A With your textbook closed, listen and take notes of the main points on a sheet of paper. Then open your textbooks and try to answer the questions. Listen again and check your answers. Correct any mistakes and add any new answers. Then share your answers with a partner or in a small group.

Tip: Difficult words and phrases are often explained in context.

What do these words mean?

chromosomes

metabolism

1 What did Jeanne Calment and Jiroemon Kimura have in common?

_____

2 What explains the longer lifespan of women?

_____

3 Why do the Japanese live longer than people elsewhere?

_____

4 How has their diet changed in recent years?

_____

5 How has that affected their health?

_____

6 What other factors can influence how long we will live?

_____

7 What can we do to break Jeanne Calment's record?

_____

8 How long can a tortoise live?

_____

9 What accounts for such a long life?

_____

B Present a short summary of what you have found out.

4 | Read and Share   Longevity

Form a small group. Each member will choose one reading passage. Read yours carefully and be ready to present and explain it. The other members will listen and take notes without looking at the reading passages. After each presentation, they will report what they have found out. The presenter will add anything they overlooked and correct any misunderstandings.

Life Expectancy in Okinawa

Blue Zones

Long Life in Monaco

How to Live to 120

5 | Discussion

Discuss the following questions with a partner or in a small group.

- The next generation of Okinawans may have a shorter lifespan. Why?
- What could your hometown or prefecture do in order to be ranked top for life expectancy?
- Would you like to live in a Longevity Blue Zone?

6 | Project   Aging Society: Problems and Solutions

A Discuss the following questions in your group and take notes on all of your ideas.

1 Japan has an aging problem. As the number of people over 65 years old grows, the overall cost to the nation of the pension system and medical care increases. What should be done to
   a) reduce these costs?
   b) to get more money to pay for them?

2 At the same time, the decline in the birth rate means there will be fewer young workers paying into the pension fund.
   a) Why has the birth rate declined?
   b) What should be done to increase it?

3 What impact would a higher birth rate have on
   a) the overall cost of pensions and healthcare in 60 years' time?
   b) Japan's ability to feed its population? (Currently 60% of food is imported.)

B When you have finished, share your answers and ideas with other groups.

7 | Listening Students' Project Reports 🎧 DL 120~123 ◎ CD2-65 ~ ◎ CD2-68

A Listen and take short notes.

Kaori

Tomohiro

Rena

Takeshi

B Share and discuss your notes with a partner or in a small group. Then discuss the ideas expressed in the Students' Project Reports.

Fill each space with a suitable word or phrase from this unit. You may need to change some words so that they fit grammatically. Not all of the answers are in the Words in Context section.

1 He claims to have cured his .... by eating nothing but soup for three months.

2 Please bring two .... copies of your passport photo.

3 On her 100th birthday, she became a ....

4 She .... her success to her own efforts.

5 The .... you get from your parents before you're born can decide your future.

6 When my grandfather died, all I .... from him was his stamp collection.

7 At the age of 65, she .... , and began to receive a monthly pension from the government.

8 It has been suggested that men die earlier than women because of their ....

9 Smoking is usually .... cancer, but it causes other serious diseases as well.

10 Bears can sleep right through the winter, thanks to their unique ....

9 | Writing

Find out about a country other than your own that is dealing with low birth rates and an aging population, and write a report.

Read and Share –Key to reading passages

Instructions for Read and Share section

The main aim of this section is to practice presentation, conversation management and note-taking. Students will work in groups of 3 to 5 members. In each Read and Share section, there are some short readings related to the theme of the unit. For example, Unit 1 has four topics. Each member of the group will choose a different reading. (If the number of members doesn't match the number of readings, some students can work with two readings, or some readings can be skipped.)

There are two formats.
Presentation (e.g. Unit 1)
Each student will study a topic and then present it, with pauses for the other members to take short notes. The other students will then summarize what they have found out and the presenter will correct any mistakes.
Q & A (Units 3, 5, 7 and 8)
Each student will study a topic and then answer questions about that topic from the other members. The other students will write the answers. Using those answers, they will then summarize what they have found out.

With both formats, students will need to be ready to explain not only the content but also the language, using paraphrase, explaining unfamiliar words, and so on.

Try to use these expressions.
Presenters:
I'm going to tell you about ...
Did you understand?
Would you like me to repeat that?
In other words, ...
Do you have any questions?
So what did you find out from my presentation?

Other members:
Could you say that again, please?
Excuse me. Could you speak more slowly, please?
Could we have a little more time to write the answers?
What did you say about ...?
Did you say ...?

1 The 'r's of Garbage Management (Unit 1)

People often talk about the three 'r's of waste management: **reduce**, **reuse**, and **recycle**. That means we should reduce the amount of stuff we buy and use, reuse things such as supermarket bags, and recycle drink cans and other containers. But there are more 'r's that can help us improve our garbage management. For example, we can **repair** things like broken umbrellas (or get them repaired), we can **recharge** our batteries instead of buying new ones, and we can **refill** our ballpoint pens instead of buying new ones. And what can we do with old houses instead of demolishing them? **Renovate** them. It saves money and resources. We should also **refrain** from buying disposable goods, and **reject** pressure from the advertising industry to buy stuff we don't need. And of course, we must **refuse** the plastic bags offered by supermarket clerks. Above all, waste management has to do with our attitudes. We must **resolve** to live more sustainably, **redefine** happiness in a way that includes having less stuff, and **respect** the environment!

2 Copenhagen (Unit 2)

Copenhagen is a relatively small city with a big ambition: to be carbon-neutral before 2030. During the period from 2005 to 2015, they cut their emissions by over 40%. The city's electricity comes from a power station that burns wood chips (a renewable resource) and from an incinerator which is so clean that it has a park on top. Waste heat from the power station is used to heat 98% of all homes. 58% of their garbage is recycled—98% if you include what's burned to produce electricity. Most buses are electric, but 55% of the city's residents cycle every day. There are over 360 kilometers of bicycle-only routes. Less than 30% of all households own a car. 25% of the food sold is organic, and there are many vegan and vegetarian restaurants. Several have their own kitchen gardens or rooftop farms. A lot of the residents live in co-housing communities, where they share a garden and other amenities.

3 Solar Energy (Unit 3)

Solar energy comes from the sun. It can be produced in several ways. One method involves panels of photovoltaic (PV) cells that convert sunlight to electricity. Solar panels have been installed on millions of homes around the world. They're also used in solar power stations. For example, the Bhadla Solar Park in India can generate as much as 2,245 MW*. Another kind of solar power station uses large mirrors to reflect sunlight onto pipes containing oil. This creates intense heat which is then converted to electricity. The Noor solar power station in Morocco is the largest of this type. Energy from the sun is clean and safe, it costs nothing, and there's an infinite supply. Although it's not available at night, or during bad weather, it can now be stored in various ways for use any time. Solar energy used to be very expensive, but it's now one of the cheapest sources of energy for many countries.

*1,000 watts = 1 KW (kilowatt)   1,000 KW = 1 MW (megawatt)
 1,000 MW = 1 GW (gigawatt)   1,000 GW = 1 TW (terawatt)

4 Renewable Energy (Unit 4)

Climate change is caused by greenhouse gases emitted when burning fossil fuels for energy. We can stop these emissions by using renewable energy instead, such as wind and solar energy. To speed up the transition, we need to stop giving the fossil fuel industry subsidies and instead subsidize investment in clean energy. One of the biggest sources of carbon is cars, buses and trucks. We need to give drivers incentives to switch to electric vehicles, like they do in Norway. Of course, the electricity used to charge the car batteries must come from clean energy too. As for heavy vehicles like buses and trucks, we'll need to use biofuels for a while, but some are already using clean hydrogen produced by electrolysis using only renewable energy and water.

5 Black Rhinoceros (Unit 5)

There are two main species of rhinoceros living in Africa: white and black. Black rhinos live mainly in Namibia, Kenya and South Africa. The main threat is poaching. People in China and Vietnam will pay a lot of money for their horns, which are used to make medicine. In the 1960s there were over 70,000, but the population decreased to around 2,500 by 1990. The international trade was banned in 1977, but they continue to be sold on the black market. In 2014, an attempt was made to save them by cutting off their horns, as a rhino without horns is of no interest to a poacher. It was effective and caused no harm to the rhinos, except that they tended to avoid other rhinos. Now there are three main approaches for saving them: efforts to catch poachers using advanced technology, translocation to areas with smaller populations, and captive breeding.

6 Payment for Ecosystem Services (Unit 6)

A lot of research has been done that shows tropical rainforests are worth more when used sustainably than when turned into palm oil plantations or cattle ranches. In Costa Rica, the government realized that the supply of clean water and healthy rivers depended on rainforests. They introduced a system of Payment for Ecosystem Services in which landowners were paid to maintain their forests. The money came from water and power companies that depended on a steady supply of water, and also from a tax on gasoline. The landowners were also encouraged to engage in sustainable farming, growing fruit, vegetables, coffee, spices, medicinal plants, and so on. The area of tropical rainforest has increased from 21% in 1987 to about 75% today. Payment for ecosystem services is a great way to save rainforests.

7 Runa Tupari (Unit 7)

Runa Tupari is a travel agency in Otavalo, Ecuador, run by and for indigenous people living in nearby villages. It was set up in 2001 with help from a Dutch farmers' association. The program aimed to provide a sustainable income to local communities and a chance for tourists to experience life in a Quechua community. It offers homestays in nearby villages, guided nature tours and treks to nearby lakes and mountains, cultural tours and farm visits. The homestay hosts, guides, taxi drivers, artisans and vendors in the Otavalo market all earn money from tourists, and get a chance to meet people from many countries. The program has greatly improved living standards in each rural community and also raised the self-esteem of the local people.

8 Hunger (Unit 8)

About 800 million people around the world are suffering from chronic hunger. The main cause of hunger is poverty. Many people just don't have enough money to buy the food they need. But there are other factors besides poverty. A lot of food is wasted because of poor distribution and storage. A lot more is fed to animals. That's very wasteful: if we all stopped eating meat, we could probably feed at least five times as many people. And while many people don't get enough to eat, even more people eat too much. The World Food Program (WFP) can help in the short term by distributing surplus food to where it's most needed, but to solve the problem of hunger in the long term, we have to eliminate poverty. That requires sustainable development. Promoting family planning may also help: fewer children means less mouths to feed. And we need to eat less meat and stop wasting food.

9 ICAN: the International Campaign to Abolish Nuclear Weapons (Unit 9)

Since the first test of a nuclear weapon in 1945, people have been calling for them to be banned. So far, numerous international treaties have been adopted that are aimed at ending the testing and proliferation of nuclear weapons, and at least six Nobel Peace Prize awards have been related to the anti-nuclear movement, but until 2021, the only actual bans on nuclear weapons were regional (Latin America and Antarctica), in space and on the seabed. But thanks to the efforts of the International Campaign to Abolish Nuclear Weapons and of many other NGOs, the UN finally adopted the Treaty on the Prohibition of Nuclear Weapons in 2017. The treaty came into force on 22 January 2021. Regrettably, of the 15 nations that currently have nuclear weapons, none has agreed to phase them out.

10 A Refugee Weightlifter (Unit 10)

Cyrille Tchatchet II, a weightlifter, came to the UK from Cameroon to compete for his country in the 2014 Commonwealth Games, but disappeared. After living on the street for a long time, he was picked up by the police and taken to a detention center. An NGO helped him apply for refugee status. While waiting, he got a Refugee Athlete Scholarship from the International Olympic Committee and started weightlifting again. In 2020 he accepted an invitation to compete in the 2020 Olympics as a member of the Refugee Olympic Team. He didn't win a medal, but he eventually got a job and was granted permanent residence in the UK.

11 UNICEF (Unit 11)

The United Nations Children's Fund (UNICEF) was established in 1950 to provide healthcare and education to children affected by war and poverty. Since then, it has dealt with many other emergencies besides war, including the worldwide coronavirus pandemic and the impacts of climate change such as the severe floods in Pakistan in 2022. UNICEF distributes vaccines for various diseases including cholera, malaria and Ebola. In addition to saving the lives of over 50 million children, UNICEF led a campaign which resulted in the 1989 Convention on the Rights of the Child. UNICEF was awarded the Nobel Peace Prize in 1965. Its headquarters are in New York.

12 Martin Luther King Jr. (Unit 12)

In 1955, a black woman was arrested on a bus for sitting in a seat reserved for whites. Martin Luther King Jr., the pastor of a local Baptist church, organized a boycott of the bus company that lasted 382 days. He was arrested and his home was attacked with a bomb, but the boycott succeeded. Soon after that, the US Supreme Court ruled that segregation was unconstitutional. In 1957, King became the leader of a new civil rights campaign. He was arrested many times, but at last his campaign was successful. In 1963, he led a march to Washington D.C. and gave a speech to a huge audience. He talked of his dream for an America where all races were treated equally. In the following year, the Civil Rights Act was passed, and later, the Voting Rights Act. King was awarded the Nobel Peace Prize in 1964. Tragically, he was assassinated four years later.

13 Maria Montessori (Unit 13)

Maria Montessori grew up in Italy. In high school, she wanted to become an engineer, but changed her mind and became the only female medical student at the University of Rome. Her early research focused on educating children with intellectual disabilities. After graduating, she started a school for children living in a poor neighborhood in Rome. She developed innovative methods, materials and activities, and a deep understanding of how children develop intellectually. Her materials for reading development were particularly effective, and the children's ability to read and write was far above average for their age. Her reputation spread, and she was invited to give lectures and open Montessori schools all over the world. As she grew older, she began to focus on peace education and on children's rights.

14 Life Expectancy in Okinawa (Unit 14)

Japan has over 61,000 people who are at least one hundred years old. Many of them live in Okinawa, a place famous for its long life expectancy. Why do Okinawans live so long? There are four main reasons. The first is their traditional diet. It's low-calorie, low-fat, low-protein and high in carbohydrates, with lots of vegetables and soy-based foods. The second factor is their relaxed, low-stress lifestyles. On the other hand, they remain active even when they're old. The fourth reason for their long lives is their close relationships with family and community. But diets and lifestyles in Okinawa have changed. It isn't even Japan's top prefecture for life expectancy any more: in 2023 it was ranked 3rd for women and 30th for men.

15 Used Electrical Appliances (Unit 1)

Until 2001, Japanese manufacturers had little interest in what happened to their products after they broke down. But then the government introduced strict recycling regulations making the manufacturers responsible for proper disposal of unwanted air conditioners, TVs, refrigerators and washing machines. Computers were added to the list in 2003. As recycling technology developed, it became possible to cut costs, and eventually it was cheaper to recycle than to import some of the metals needed. It was also better for the environment. For example, cellphones contain coltan, which is mined in Africa. The mines are very poorly regulated, and the natural environment is destroyed. But now coltan and other important minerals such as gold and copper can be recovered from old cellphones and other devices. What's more, some researchers think the world's largest supply of valuable metals may actually be in Japan's old landfills.

16 Oslo (Unit 2)

Oslo's main climate goal is to cut its overall carbon emissions to zero by 2030. The city is lucky enough to be the capital of Norway, a country that gets 98.5% of its electricity from hydropower and wind, and has enough leftover to sell to its neighbors. The city's trams and metro are electric, and from 2025, all new cars sold in Norway must be electric. Of course, all the electricity used by cars will be from renewable energy, but the buses will run on biogas made from food waste. Biomass plants also provide district heating for homes. Much of Oslo's waste is recycled. The rest is burned in incinerators that don't emit greenhouse gases because they use carbon capture and storage. Oslo was chosen as the European Green Capital in 2017, and one reason was the fact that 72% of the city is green space. This is said to be the highest proportion in the world for a capital city.

17 Geothermal Energy (Unit 3)

Geothermal energy comes from underground heat. Hot springs are common in Japan and many other countries. They're a natural form of geothermal energy. Where there are no hot springs, underground heat can be harnessed by drilling a hole and pumping hot water up. It can be used for district heating or converted to electricity. The world's first geothermal power station was built in Italy in 1911. Now there are many around the world. For example, Iceland gets about 70% of all its energy from geothermal sources. That includes electricity generation, district heating, swimming pools, greenhouses and even fish farms. Geothermal energy is clean and safe, and the resource itself costs almost nothing. However, getting it from under the ground can be quite expensive, depending on how far down it is.

18 Plant-based Diets (Unit 4)

Agriculture is one of the biggest sources of greenhouse gases, and much of this comes from livestock farming. Meat and dairy products account for over 14% of all greenhouse gas emissions. By switching to plant-based diets we can cut over 10% of these emissions and also enjoy better health. But for people who love meat too much to give it up, there are now meat alternatives. Some are plant-based but taste just like meat, and they can be made using a 3D printer! Others are made from animal cells cultivated in a laboratory, but don't involve harming animals, which should please vegetarians and vegans. We can also produce meat from bacteria, rather like making beer from yeast. And finally, we can now produce flour made from bugs and use it to make very nutritious burgers.

19 California Condor (Unit 5)

The California condor is North America's largest bird. It has a 3-meter wing span and weighs up to 12 kilograms. Condors live mostly in mountainous areas of California and Arizona. They eat dead animals such as sheep, deer and even bears. Their population declined due to the use of chemicals by farmers and collisions with electric power lines. They also suffered lead poisoning after eating animals that had been shot by hunters. By 1987, they were almost extinct in the wild, so the last 27 were captured for captive breeding programs. These were successful, and by 2022 there were 336 in the wild and about 200 in captivity. But their status remains critically endangered, according to the IUCN.

20 Ecotourism (Unit 6)

Costa Rica is the world's leading ecotourism destination. The government understood that tourists (both foreign and domestic) wanted to explore the rainforests and see many of the fascinating creatures that live there. So they made a great effort to restore their rainforests. As a result, the tourism industry grew, and many jobs were created for hotel workers, tour guides, restaurant employees, taxi drivers and so on. Costa Rica also has beautiful beaches, so tourists could enjoy many different activities during their trip. It's only a small country, but its sustainable tourism policy has had a big impact on other countries too.

21 Tumani Tenda (Unit 7)

Tumani Tenda is a village in the Gambia, West Africa. The local community discussed whether or not to cut down the nearby rainforest in order to grow more crops. They decided instead to protect the forest. This decision won them an environmental award, and they used the money to build a camp for ecotourists, consisting of traditional huts and a restaurant. It's located about 500 meters from the village, but tourists are welcome to take part in village life, farming and fishing. Profits from the community-owned ecotourism camp have paid for a school, a bakery, a chicken farm and a generator.

22 Disease (Unit 8)

Each year, around five million children, mostly in low-income countries, die before their fifth birthday. Their deaths are mainly due to disease. In most cases, dirty water is to blame. Many lives could be saved by providing access to safe drinking water and improved sanitation. According to some estimates, this would cost about $150 billion a year, but the benefits would be much greater. Disease is also linked to malnutrition. When children don't have enough to eat, they easily get sick and it's harder for them to recover. Providing free school lunches can help address this problem. Poor countries also need help in vaccinating every child against common diseases. Many can't afford these simple solutions, so rich countries should help, by providing funding through UNICEF and similar organizations.

23 WFP: the World Food Program (Unit 9)

Sustainable Development Goal Number Two is zero hunger. That's a major challenge, and it's getting harder every year, due to climate change, war and the constant increase in population. Making sure everyone has enough to eat is the job of the WFP, which was established in 1961. They do that by providing food to victims of famine caused by floods, droughts and other natural disasters. They also help farmers to restore degraded farmland and repair necessary infrastructure such as irrigation canals. In addition, they provide school meals, using food grown by local farmers. The WFP has set up early warning systems to warn of extreme weather events such as the cyclones that hit the Philippines every year. Lastly, they have encouraged and helped smallholder African farmers to register their ownership of land. The WFP was awarded the Nobel Peace Prize in 2020.

24 Refugee Musicians (Unit 10)

Among the millions of refugees seeking safety in various places, there have been many musicians, including Frederic Chopin and Freddie Mercury. The Eurovision Song Contest of 2021 featured two former refugees. Toussaint Chiza, from the Republic of Congo, represented Sweden, while Manizha Sangin, from Tajikistan, represented Russia. Chiza, who spent three years in a refugee camp before moving to Sweden, was very popular. So was Sangin until she released an anti-war song criticizing the Russian invasion of Ukraine. After that, she lost many of her Russian fans. She had good reasons for hating war: she herself left her country to escape from conflict. Neither Chiza nor Sangin won the contest, but they both showed how refugees can contribute to society.

25 UNESCO (Unit 11)

What do the Taj Mahal, the Grand Canyon and Himeji Castle have in common? They're all World Heritage sites. Protecting over 1,000 cultural and natural heritage sites is just one of UNESCO's many responsibilities. UNESCO stands for the United Nations Education, Scientific and Cultural Organization, and their work involves promoting education, science and culture throughout the world. Thanks to UNESCO's literacy campaigns, many adults have learned to read and write; and in most developing countries, the proportion of children going to school has increased. UNESCO is also involved in many scientific projects including one aimed at finding out what the universe is made of and how it works. They also support intangible cultural heritage such as Japanese bunraku and protect languages at risk of dying out, including Ainu. UNESCO's headquarters are in Paris.

26 Peter Benenson (Unit 12)

In 1961, two Portuguese students in a bar called for democracy. They were arrested and thrown in jail. A British lawyer named Peter Benenson read about this and was shocked. He established an organization to campaign for the release of political prisoners, and called it Amnesty International. It's now the world's largest human rights organization. It has helped many thousands of political prisoners to gain their freedom, and has increased awareness of human rights worldwide. In 1977, Amnesty was awarded the Nobel Peace Prize. Its staff, members, supporters and activists all over the world monitor human rights and report on abuses. They use social media to raise public awareness and put pressure on governments and corporations to address serious human rights concerns.

27 Malala Yousafzai (Unit 13)

Malala lived in a small town in Northern Pakistan. Her father was a teacher, and he believed girls should receive the same education as boys. But some men with extreme ideas about religion invaded the area and banned girls from attending school. From the age of 11, Malala began campaigning for girls to be allowed to study. Her blog was published by the BBC, and she became famous. In 2012, she was on her school bus when it was stopped by extremists and she was shot in the head. She was flown to a hospital in the UK and managed to recover from her injury. It was too dangerous to return to Pakistan, so she continued her campaign from the UK. On her 15th birthday, she gave a powerful speech at the United Nations in New York. In 2014, at the age of 17, she became the youngest person to be awarded the Nobel Peace Prize.

28 Blue Zones (Unit 14)

About 20 years ago, a Belgian researcher discovered an area in Sardinia with many centenarians. He drew a circle around the area on a map using a blue pen. This was the first of five Blue Zones. It has the world's highest proportion of men over 100 years old. They eat a low-protein diet and lead very active lives. Another Blue Zone is an island in Greece called Ikaria. People there eat a traditional Mediterranean diet with lots of vegetables eaten fresh or with olive oil. A third Blue Zone is a religious community in California named Loma Linda. They're vegetarians. They don't smoke or drink alcohol, and most avoid coffee too. The fourth Blue Zone is the Nicoya Peninsula in Costa Rica. They have the world's lowest death rate for people of middle age. Okinawa is the fifth Blue Zone.

29 Paper (Unit 1)

As you probably know, most paper is made from wood pulp, which comes from trees. In Japan, about 80% of all waste paper is recycled. That's important for three reasons. First, to produce new paper, trees have to be cut. Cutting trees and not replacing them is one cause of climate change. Second, making new paper uses a lot more energy than recycling it. Third, when paper is burned, it emits harmful gases such as chlorine. So why don't we recycle all of our paper? For one thing, the fibers in the pulp become weaker each time it's recycled. For another, it's difficult and expensive to recycle certain kinds of paper products, such as paper cups and photos. A further problem is that it often costs less to import cheap virgin pulp from countries such as Indonesia than to recycle paper in Japan. We should at least make sure that our paper comes from sustainably-managed forests.

30 Freiburg (Unit 2)

Freiburg is said to be the greenest city in Germany. It all began in 1975 when residents opposed a decision to build a nuclear power plant nearby. Various environmental institutes were created, and a cluster of green businesses developed, focusing on energy, architecture, services, and environmental protection. The world's first carbon-negative house was built here. Freiburg has 400 kilometers of bicycle paths, and 40% of the town is forest, certified by the Forest Stewardship Council (FSC). That forest has Germany's tallest tree: 63 meters tall. There are about 22,000 trees along the streets. The city center is car-free. Freiburg has more solar panels than any other city in Germany, despite only having 230,000 residents. One goal is for all of their electricity to be from renewable sources by 2035.

31 Tidal Energy (Unit 3)

Tidal energy comes from the twice-daily rise and fall of the sea level. It can be harnessed by building a dam on a narrow estuary where there's a great difference between high and low tide. Each day, the dam is closed at high tide, trapping sea water behind it. As the sea level falls in front of the dam, water behind the dam is released through turbines, producing electricity. Tidal power stations can exploit the incoming flow from the rising tide as well. The world's first commercial tidal power station was built on the Rance estuary in Northern France in 1966. It can generate 240 megawatts. The largest now is the Sihwa Lake power station (254 megawatts) in South Korea, but much bigger ones have been proposed, such as Penzhina Bay, Russia (87 gigawatts). Tidal power stations are expensive to build, and have a significant impact on the tidal environment; but tidal energy itself is free, unlimited, safe to produce and reliable. Moreover, it emits no greenhouse gases.

32 Planting Trees (Unit 4)

As you know, forests are an important carbon sink. But a lot of the world's forests have been cut down or burned. That must stop. The more trees we lose, the harder it will be to stop climate change. We need much stricter penalties for unsustainable logging. But that's not enough; we also need to plant trees—billions of them. There are some very ambitious projects now, including several that aim to plant a trillion trees, although it's not clear if there's enough space to do that. There would be enough space if we all stopped eating meat. Some researchers say we don't even need to plant trees, they'll grow on their own if we let them.

33 Polar Bear (Unit 5)

Polar bears live on coasts and islands within the Arctic region of Alaska, Canada, Greenland, Norway and Russia. Estimates of their population vary from 22,000 to 31,000. A decline of 30% is expected by 2050. The main threat is global warming. They need sea ice for walking around, hunting, resting and mating, but the ice is melting earlier each year. The bears can't get enough to eat, so they approach towns looking for food, and sometimes have to be shot. Hunting is legal, although there are quotas. Another problem is pollution caused by oil leaking from oil wells and ships, and harmful chemicals brought by ocean currents. Tourism is a problem too, as it disturbs the bears and causes stress. In 1973, an international agreement was made to protect polar bears and their habitats. But unless global warming is stopped, the polar bear will eventually become extinct.

34 Carbon Offsets (Unit 6)

An indigenous Brazilian tribe named the Surui live in a 248,000 hectare rainforest. A young chief wanted to protect the forest from illegal mining and logging. In 2007, he asked Google to map the territory. Then he invited UN experts to estimate how much carbon the forest was taking in from the atmosphere. To everyone's surprise, it was 200,000 tonnes a year. Then a cosmetics company offered to pay the Surui a large sum of money to offset its own carbon emissions. The money was used for community health and education projects. About one quarter of all carbon stored in and under tropical forests is on land occupied by indigenous tribes, who live sustainably. But although 188 countries signed the Paris Agreement on Global Warming, only 21 of those countries recognized indigenous land rights. It's really important for the land rights of indigenous tribes to be guaranteed worldwide.

35 REST (Unit 7)

The Responsible Ecological Social Tours Project (REST) was established to enable rural communities in Thailand to manage and benefit from sustainable tourism. REST has helped to set up homestays in farming and fishing villages, with cultural experiences including boat trips, nature walks, treks, handicraft demonstrations and other activities. These provide small groups of tourists with opportunities to get to know the local people and their culture. The local communities have a chance to earn extra income that helps pay for children's education and medical costs, and also roads and wells. The project was so successful that REST was asked to set up similar projects in neighboring countries.

36 Illiteracy (Unit 8)

About one in five African children don't attend school. As a result, they're unable to read or write. This limits their chances of finding a proper job and contributing to the national economy. The main cause of poor school attendance is poverty. Many children are unable to go to school because they have to work to support their families, or because of the cost of school fees, books, uniforms, transportation and so on. One solution is for rich countries to provide grants or interest-free loans to the poorest countries in order to subsidize free primary education, which is supposed to be a basic human right. Another solution is to persuade parents to send their children to school by providing free lunches. These policies are especially effective in the case of girls, as the higher their education level, the fewer children they themselves have. By investing more in education, poor countries can greatly reduce illiteracy and achieve faster economic growth.

37 MSF: Médecins Sans Frontières (Unit 9)

MSF was established in 1971 after a brutal civil war in Nigeria. They work in about 70 countries, including conflict zones and areas struck by natural disasters such as earthquakes and hurricanes. They also operate where dangerous diseases such as Ebola are spreading rapidly. Their staff consists of around 45,000 skilled workers, including doctors, nurses and experts in logistics. Where there's civil war, they treat victims on both sides. They refuse to accept any funding from governments, in order to be seen as neutral and to be free to criticize government policies that may exacerbate the problems, such as during the terrible famine in Ethiopia in 1985. Their work is often very dangerous, and sometimes their workers are killed. In 1999, they were awarded the Nobel Peace Prize.

38 Refugee Farmers (Unit 10)

For years, African migrants have paid smugglers to take them to Europe, where they hoped to find work. The journey is dangerous, and thousands have drowned while crossing the Mediterranean Sea. One of the main entry points for illegal immigration is Lampedusa Island in Italy. From there, many migrants went to places like Rosarno, where they can find low-paid jobs on farms. In 2010, after an attack on African migrants in Rosarno, some moved to Rome and applied for a humanitarian residence permit. When they got their permits, a group formed a food cooperative, rented a farm and began producing fruit, organic vegetables and yoghurt. They delivered their products by bicycle, and became very popular during the coronavirus lockdown. They originally came from Mali, Nigeria, Benin and Gambia. They named their cooperative Barikama, meaning *resistance* in the Malian language.

39 FAO (Unit 11)

The United Nations Food and Agriculture Organization was founded in 1945 with the aim of improving living standards in rural areas, increasing farm production, improving food distribution and raising nutrition levels. It's based in Rome, but much of its work is carried out in developing countries, where it coordinates the distribution of food aid through the World Food Program and supervises agricultural research. One of its major achievements was the Green Revolution, which led to a big increase in the production of rice and cereals in Asia. A big concern now is future food shortages as world population grows and agricultural productivity declines. The FAO says we must give up eating meat because it accounts for over 14% of global warming.

40 Craig Kielburger (Unit 12)

In Pakistan and India, many children are forced to work in factories like slaves, even though this is illegal. It's called bonded labor. In 1996, one boy, named Iqbal Masih, escaped and told his story to the mass media. Soon after, he was murdered. A Canadian boy aged 12 named Craig Kielburger read a report about this in his local newspaper and was shocked. He researched the situation and found out there were about 250 million children like Iqbal in South Asia. He set up an NGO called Free the Children. They campaigned against bonded labor and gathered money to help the children. They built a rehabilitation center in India, enabled children in factories to have lunch each day and go to school, and provided sewing machines to families so they could earn enough money without having their children work.

41 Marie Curie (Unit 13)

Marie Curie was a great scientist. She was the first person to win two Nobel Prizes, and in two different categories. She was born in Poland, but women there couldn't attend university, so she went to Paris to study. In 1896, she began to research uranium. This led to her discovery of two new elements, which she named polonium and radium. She found that radium destroyed cancerous cells faster than normal cells and realized it could be used to treat cancer. When war broke out in 1914, she created mobile radiology units to help doctors treat injured soldiers, and became head of the Red Cross radiology division. She refused to patent her process for isolating radium in order to allow others to do further research. She was awarded the 1903 Nobel Prize for physics, which she shared with her husband and Henri Becquerel, and the Nobel Prize for chemistry for her discovery of polonium and radium.

42 Long Life in Monaco (Unit 14)

The average life expectancy in Japan is high, but it's not the world's highest. That's in Monaco, a tiny country located next to southern France, close to the Italian border. The average person there now is expected to live for almost 90 years. Why do the people of Monaco live so long? One reason might be the mild climate. Another might be the famous Mediterranean diet. But more importantly, a lot of people living in Monaco are very wealthy. In fact, 30% of the population are millionaires. So they can afford the best medical care. And nobody pays tax in Monaco, so they don't have to worry about that. On the other hand, Monaco is also the world's most crowded country, so we might expect the people living there to get stressed out occasionally.

43 Drink Containers (Unit 1)

Drinks can be sold in PET bottles, metal cans, glass bottles and paper packs. Manufacturers like PET bottles because they're strong, light and cheap to make. About seven billion are used every year in Japan, and approximately 95% are recycled. That's good, because a lot of energy is needed to make them, and they're hard to get rid of. They release harmful gases when burned and take a long time to degrade in landfills. Metal cans are also popular, especially in vending machines, and the recycling rate for them is high too. On the other hand, glass bottles are heavy and break easily, so they tend to be used mostly for alcoholic drinks and expensive cooking oil. Products such as milk and fruit juice are commonly sold in paper packages, and these also have high recycling rates. But as recycling technology improves, we should be able to achieve 100% recycling rates for all drink containers in order to protect the environment and save resources.

44 Vienna (Unit 2)

Vienna is often described as the world's most livable city. It's also one of the most sustainable. First, it's very green: around half of the city consists of woods, fields, parks, gardens, lawns and even vineyards. There's also a large natural wetland with over 100 kinds of birds. Second, the city has an excellent public transportation network carrying 966 million passengers a year on trams, metro and buses covering the entire city. There are 1,400 kilometers of bicycle-friendly routes. And Vienna is an extremely walkable city. So most people don't need a car. But for anyone who does, there are over 1,850 charging stations for electric vehicles. Actually, Vienna's first electric car was introduced in 1899! Third, with around 800 farms within the city, Vienna can produce a lot of food with zero food miles. There are also many local farmers' markets. Fourth, 65% of all municipal waste is recycled. Some is transformed into electricity in an incinerator that's a very popular tourist attraction owing to its unique design. Vienna is a very green city.

45 Wind Energy (Unit 3)

Wind energy is made by using the wind to turn blades attached to a turbine. Wind turbines can be erected on land or offshore. Denmark gets about 40% of its electricity from wind farms. The world's biggest wind farm is in India. It can produce 1,600 megawatts. A much bigger one is under development in Gansu, China (20 gigawatts). Wind energy is clean, safe and renewable; and the wind itself is free. Wind farms can be built on ordinary farmland (providing farmers with extra income), but are only cost-effective if there's plenty of wind. Local residents complain about the noise made by wind turbines; and some conservationists oppose wind turbines because they spoil the view, and sometimes kill migrating birds. However, these impacts are a small price to pay for technology that can help us stop climate change.

46 CCS: Carbon Capture and Storage (Unit 4)

It'll be easier to meet our goal of net zero carbon emissions by 2050 if we introduce technology for capturing carbon at power stations and pumping it underground. At present, this approach is used to force more oil out of old wells, and the extra oil just adds to our carbon emissions. But engineers in Iceland have found that if you pump carbon into layers of basalt, it turns into rock within a couple of years. That's a permanent solution, but it's expensive. Why not use the carbon instead to make something useful, such as concrete blocks, soft drinks or even diamonds? That's what some people are now doing. It's also possible to capture carbon straight from the air. That's called Direct Air Capture, and it can be done anywhere in the world.

47 Mountain Gorilla (Unit 5)

Mountain gorillas live in the forests of the Virunga Mountains in Central Africa. There are gorilla communities in three countries: Uganda, Rwanda and the Democratic Republic of Congo. Now, their population is fairly stable, but at one time it was thought they might become extinct. The main threats were the creation of new settlements and farms in the area, the production of charcoal for cooking, animal traps set by hunters, and diseases such as Ebola spread by humans. The first real effort to protect the gorillas was the establishment of the Virunga National Park in 1925, but by the 1970s it had become a very dangerous place due to conflicts between government soldiers and rebel armies. Since then, security has been improved and tourism has increased. Gorilla tours are popular, and they provide income for the local communities.

48 Debt-for-Nature Agreements (Unit 6)

Bolivia is a poor country with huge forests and high biodiversity. But the government borrowed too much money from international banks and couldn't pay it back. And the debt kept growing. In 1987, one of the world's biggest conservation organizations offered to repay some of Bolivia's debts in exchange for the right to manage a large area of tropical forest. The government agreed, the money was paid, the forest was protected and a new debt-for-nature funding model was established. Since then, there have been many more, with a total value of more than $1 billion, and they have involved not just conservation groups but governments as well. Could your government save tropical rainforests around the world through debt-for-nature agreements?

49 Chalalan Ecolodge (Unit 7)

Chalalan Ecolodge is located in the Bolivian rainforest, and is run by an indigenous community. It was built with two goals: to protect the rainforest and to provide a sustainable income for the local people. Since it opened for business, it has attracted a steady stream of ecotourists, and has earned thousands of dollars. It's considered to be among the top ten ecotourism destinations in the world, and has appeared in several TV documentaries. The nearby river and surrounding area are full of fascinating species of animals, insects, birds and plants. Thanks partly to the Chalalan project, the rainforest has been protected from development.

50 Unemployment (Unit 8)

More than 70 million young people have no job, and many more work only on a temporary, seasonal or part-time basis. In many developing countries, this is due to high birth rates and slow economic growth. But it's also due to a lack of the skills needed for the jobs available in fast-growing sectors such as technology, renewable energy and tourism. This can be addressed through vocational education and training courses aimed at students of high school age. Another approach is to support new entrepreneurs with finance and expert advice. Some African countries have created regional hubs specializing in certain industries, including high-tech agriculture. Others have set up online job centers providing details of vacancies. Enabling young people to find productive employment can help to stimulate economic growth and reduce poverty.

51 ICBL: the International Campaign to Ban Landmines (Unit 9)

In many countries, landmines have been buried under the ground to deter enemies from attacking. They're cheap and effective, but they remain there long after the threat of war has ended, and their victims include many farmers and children walking to school. It's difficult and dangerous to locate and disable landmines, and very frustrating to know that new mines are being made, sold and used faster than old ones are disabled. In 1992, several organizations came together to campaign for a total ban on landmines. They were coordinated by Jody Williams. Using her networking skills and persistence, she gained support from celebrities, the Red Cross, the UN and eventually several governments. In 1997, the UN adopted the Ottawa Treaty banning the production and use of landmines. Three weeks later, Jody Williams and the International Campaign to Ban Landmines were awarded the Nobel Peace Prize.

52 A Climate Refugee? (Unit 10)

Ioane Teitiota grew up in Kiribati. He applied for a work permit in New Zealand, got a three-year visa and moved there with his family. But when the visa expired in 2010, he didn't want to leave, so he asked to be recognized as a refugee. His argument was that his country is gradually being submerged by the sea due to climate change, and that this is leading to overcrowding and a lack of fresh water. His claim wasn't accepted, because the Refugee Convention recognizes only people fleeing from persecution. After he was deported to Kiribati, he appealed to the UN Human Rights Committee. His appeal was rejected because there was no immediate threat to his life. However, the UNHRC declared that as the risks of climate change grow, countries hosting migrants from regions most at risk may no longer be allowed to send them home.

53 WHO (Unit 11)

The World Health Organization was set up in 1948, and has its headquarters in Geneva. Its main goal is to improve the health of all people, wherever they live. It has been very successful in eliminating diseases such as smallpox. It also deals with emergencies such as outbreaks of Ebola, Zika virus, dengue fever and coronavirus. It coordinates the production and distribution of vaccines and medical equipment to poor countries and the collection of data on new infections. It also researches the harmful effects of agricultural chemicals, and conducts aggressive anti-smoking campaigns. Another of its targets is obesity. It recognizes this as a serious but easily preventable disease and supports campaigns to promote healthier diets.

54 Fashion Revolution (Unit 12)

Article 23 of the Universal Declaration of Human Rights and SDG 8 both focus on decent work for everybody. But there are many people who are unable to find work, and many of those lucky enough to have a job are underpaid and work in very bad conditions. The fashion industry is a typical example. In 2013, a tall building in Dacca, Bangladesh, collapsed, killing more than a thousand workers who were producing garments for famous fashion brands. This tragedy exposed the low wages and bad working conditions in the fashion industry. Two fashion designers decided to change things. They established an NGO named Fashion Revolution with the goal of improving wages and working conditions in the fashion industry. Their campaign Who Made My Clothes and their Fashion Transparency Index have been very effective in reducing exploitation in the industry and also reducing its environmental impact.

55 Florence Nightingale (Unit 13)

Have you ever heard of Florence Nightingale? She's known as the founder of the nursing profession. She was born into a rich family, but gave up her comfortable life in order to help the sick. During the Crimean War from 1853 to 1856, many soldiers died of their injuries and also from disease. In 1854, Nightingale brought a group of 38 women to the Crimea to treat injured soldiers. She introduced new ideas that saved many lives, such as the importance of good hygiene and nutrition. She was called "the lady of the lamp" because she visited the wounded soldiers every night to check on their condition and encourage them. After the war, she established a nursing college at Saint Thomas' Hospital in London. She also wrote several influential books about medical care and hospital administration.

56 How to Live to 120 (Unit 14)

Do you want to live to the age of 120? This is what you need. The most important factor is your genes. So if any of your grandparents were healthy centenarians, you could be one too. The second factor is gender. Women live around six years longer. Whatever the reason, you have a better chance if you're a woman. The third factor is what you eat and drink. So if you love junk food, forget about becoming a centenarian. The fourth factor is your attitude to life. A positive attitude can win you an extra 10 years or more. Exercise is the next factor. Just walking a couple of kilometers a day can help you to stay healthy much longer. Another important factor is your social relationships. You need close family ties and friendly neighbors. But the final factor is the one that decides your genes and your gender: luck.

57 Hydrogen (Unit 3)

Hydrogen is the third most common element on our planet. It's in the land, the sea and the air, but always joined to other elements. There are ways to capture it for use as a source of energy, but only one of those ways doesn't involve fossil fuels. So-called "green hydrogen" is made through electrolysis of water, using electricity from clean energy sources. Why use hydrogen rather than solar or wind? Because it can be produced any time and stored until needed. What's more, it can produce the very high temperatures needed for making steel or cement. It can also be used as a fuel for heavy trucks, ships, trains and even planes. And the supply is almost unlimited. Green hydrogen is at present very expensive to produce, store and transport, but prices will come down as the technology spreads.

58 Lear's Macaw (Unit 5)

Lear's macaw is one of the world's rarest birds. It lives only on sandstone cliffs in Bahia State, Brazil, and its main food is nuts from the licuri palm. Farmers cut down many trees in order to grow crops, and killed macaws that were eating their corn. Poachers trapped the birds to sell them to collectors. Then aggressive bees began to occupy their nests. The macaws almost became extinct, but their population recovered thanks to efforts to protect them. Poaching and trafficking were banned. Their habitats were carefully monitored. Successful captive breeding programs were established in Germany and Tenerife. An NGO provided beehives to local people so that they could lure the bees away from the macaws' nests. Estimates of the present population of the birds vary from 1,120 to about 1,600. With their population growing again and too few licuri trees to feed them, the farmers are once again worried about their crops.

59 Homelessness (Unit 8)

In the Philippines, there are around 4.5 million people living on or beside the street, including 1.2 million children. Many more live in slums. The situation is similar in many other developing countries. The main reason is poverty. Many people can't afford to buy or rent a home; and as rents rise, more people become homeless. Another reason is the steady migration of people from poor villages looking for work in the cities. A third reason is high birth rates: the population is growing faster than the number of homes. Another problem is damage caused by natural disasters such as typhoons. Poverty can be addressed by stimulating economic growth in order to create jobs and raise wages. If more people can afford to buy a house, more houses will be built. But there will always be people who are desperately poor. City governments have a duty to provide temporary housing in empty buildings or in purpose-built homeless shelters.

60 UNEP (Unit 11)

The United Nations Environment Programme was established in 1972. It's concerned with protecting all aspects of the global environment. For example, it's negotiated international agreements to protect the atmosphere, such as the UN Framework Convention on Climate Change and the establishment of the IPCC in 2007, the Montreal Protocol protecting the ozone layer, and regional cooperation on reducing acid rain. It's also been active in protecting biodiversity in tropical forests and other sensitive environments. The Convention on International Trade in Endangered Species was a UNEP initiative. In 2016, UNEP warned about the risk of dangerous viruses passing from animals to humans, and just four years later, the coronavirus pandemic arrived. But UNEP's biggest achievement was the Paris Agreement of 2015 to stop global warming.

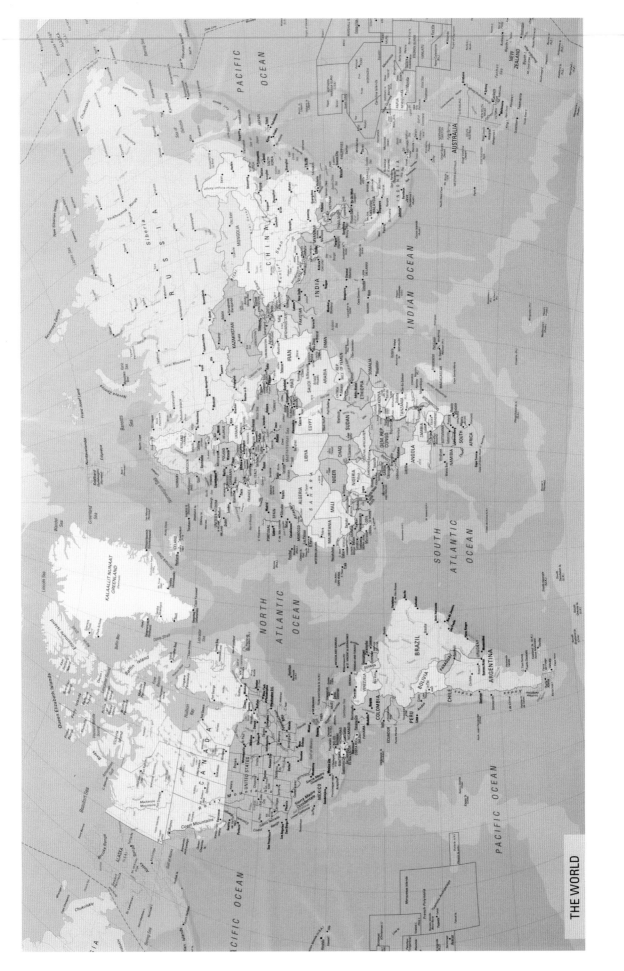

THE WORLD

本書にはCD（別売）があります

You, Me and the World
3rd Edition featuring SDGs

2024年1月20日　初版第1刷発行
2024年2月20日　初版第2刷発行

著　者　David Peaty

発行者　福　岡　正　人

発行所　株式会社　金　星　堂

（〒101-0051）東京都千代田区神田神保町3-21
Tel　（03）3263-3828（営業部）
　　　（03）3263-3997（編集部）
Fax　（03）3263-0716
https://www.kinsei-do.co.jp

編集担当　今門貴浩　　　　　　　　Printed in Japan
印刷所・製本所／シナノ書籍印刷株式会社

ISBN978-4-7647-4205-5　　C1082